HOW SWEET IT IS

JEFF JAFFE

ISBN Number 978-1-57087-774-2
Library of Congress Control Number 2011927464

Professional Press
Chapel Hill, NC 27515-4371

Manufactured in the United States of America
11 12 13 14 15   10 9 8 7 6 5 4 3 2 1

Dedicated to my Grandsons

Elliot, Matthew, Ryan, Cameron and
Great Grandson Jacob

and

Natalie and Holly

and

Bonnie and Richard

FOREWORD

Research on this book took 89 years—
—knowingly the last three.

Life is PARAGRAPHS.

Some are long and others are short. Some might be only one word. They can be interesting or boring. They can hurt or offer solace, compliment an individual or step on his toes. Paragraphs can be sad or joyful, meaningful or silly. They can be many sentences, and one or more can become a CHAPTER.

But what they all can do is to document a life and often clarify timing, emphasis, emotion, thought, actions, history, intentions and virtually every aspect of life.

Regret not the end of one. Instead, savor the promise of the next.

PARAGRAPHS are life.

One of my great regrets is that I never knew much about my grandparents and their parents. Therefore this story about my life is written in that myriad clutter of sentences, paragraphs and chapters in the hope that my grandchildren and their grandchildren will have some knowledge about me, Jeff Jaffe, and that wonderful crazy world we enjoyed so much. It is a story about my accomplishments and failures, successes and disappointments. It is a story about my era and the folks who lived, worked, suffered and laughed and, like me, enjoyed almost every moment of our lives.

Across this great and highly personal span of time, the rust of memory tends to enhance the lucky, good or prescient actions, discussions or thoughts or round the edges of spectacularly bad ones. However, any deviation from fact is purely unintentional. I have diligently tried to be fair and accurate in portraying the thoughts, actions, decisions, emotions, friends, fellow workers and events.

Looking back in time, one tends to relive the happiness of those special days when life was rich in purpose and every day was a distinct joy. I can only hope that you, dear reader, will appreciate the people and events that made life such so rich in purpose.

Palm Beach Gardens, Florida
May 2010

INTRODUCTION

The major, majestic concern of 20th century man, immediately after family—but not always—is accumulating money and possessions. The men I knew were evaluated by their NET WORTH. And their net worth was a logical outgrowth of their ambition. It is sometimes exalted, often derided, usually by the young, or those who do not have much. In the proper context it is praiseworthy, necessary, and often fun. It is life's work to some and its accumulation is the major activity of most.

This book looks at the pursuit of NET WORTH by me and a few other individuals associated with me in various enterprises. It touches on the various backgrounds of many people, as well as the sources, motivations and methods I and others used in acquiring wealth. It suggests that there was a basic modus operandi. If it could be spelled out, it would be simply "learning on the job." My life covers those tricky temptations we all experience and also mentions the character of many individuals I was fortunate to have as my associates in numerous enterprises. It relates the good and the bad, the ups and the downs, the by-roads, the fallout and the input, and gives credit to those who helped me along the business path, clearly mentioning those contributors as well as the detractors.

It is just one tiny look in a world of countless other versions.

Ideals are like the stars
We can never reach them with our hands
But like mariners at sea
We can chart our course by them.

Carl Schurz—Faneuil Hall
Boston, Mass
April 18, 1859

TABLE OF CONTENTS

CHAPTER 1

TRUE VALUE

On February 22, 1967
the Chunky Chocolate Company
was worth $10,000,000.

•

On February 23, 1967,
the next day,
it was worth $0.

Τhis was not based on some unusual financial or management problem. There was no acquisition. It was rather one of the most unusual moments of my life.

How, you may ask, can a business be worth ten million dollars one day, and worth absolutely nothing on the day following.

Based on the then current P/E formula, on February 22, 1967 the CHUNKY CHOCOLATE CORPORATION'S value, including BIT-O-HONEY, was over $10,000,000.*

WHAT HAPPENED?

Realistically there was nothing wrong with the company or its products. What occurred was something I would not wish on my worst enemy. It was, to be blunt, a federal agency that decided to stop Chunky production. That agency was the Food and Drug Administration. To this day, I will never understand why the FDA acted so rashly. The reason for such action was the possibility of Salmonella in the chocolate. But even when an independent agency proved that there was no Salmonella, the fact that a shipment, months ago, had been shipped with "possible" Salmonella, was enough to have the FDA act. There were never any instances of illnesses. Perhaps they were seeking a bigger budget. Perhaps they acted imprudently because they could run easily over a small manufacturer. Perhaps this action was part of that agency's hope to attract more news for itself. Whatever the reason, CHUNKY was vulnerable and happened to be in the middle of the road when that massive truck ran over it. It nearly destroyed a small, growing company. And it placed me in the most difficult position of my young life.

---

*$64,194,000 in 2009 dollars—AIER—American Institute of Economic Research—Conversion Factors. Appendix

CHAPTER 2

IT TOOK A WAR

| 1930-1946 |
| New York, N.Y. |

When the dark clouds of war were beginning to form in the late 1930's, and the rumblings of disaster were mounting, the candy industry was a benign and quiet splinter of the food industry. There were over 1,000 manufacturers of confectionery products—a large majority of which were small family operations.

At that time there were several important candy manufacturers such as the Hershey Chocolate Co., Peter Paul Mounds Co., Brach Candy Co., Curtiss Candy Co., Mars Candy Co., Nestle Co., and a handful of manufacturers of industrial chocolate for sale to the trade. These were all companies of long standing with well-tested operations, channels of distribution, advertising and promotion, and stable market share.

The entire industry, as well as consumers, would have to suffer through rationing of chocolate, sugar, milk and other ingredients during World War II. As supplies built up afterwards, the industry experienced tremendous demand for candy products so long denied. The major manufacturers were clearly in a position to best exploit this hunger for sweets that was evidenced by both adults and children. Most of the companies were not very aggressive, and one—Hershey—did not even advertise.

There was no candy imported from foreign manufacturers, except one exceptional idea came from England to capture an important share of the U.S. market as the fabulous M & M's.

Forest Mars, the scion of the family that owned the Mars Candy Co., had the foresight to see the great qualities of Smarties made by Rowntree & Co. of York, England. These were small ovals of chocolate coated in a thin shell of sugar in different colors and later to become famous with the slogan "melts in your mouth—not in your hand."

After World War II, the United States, acknowledged by all as the greatest country in the world, would now offer many opportunities to individuals. It provided the opportunity to achieve the American dream. Could this post-war time be an opportunity for a small company, especially since it was not even in active operation? The answer was clear and obvious.

It is possible.
Anything which is not impossible is possible.
This is possible.

—Vincent Lardo

CHAPTER 3

ANCESTORS

> **May 1883**
> **Buttenhausen, Germany**
> **July 1889**
> **Lithuania**

It's a long way from a ghetto in Lithuania to a modest town—Buttenhausen—in Germany in the 1880's. Not just in miles, but more distinctively in background, culture, language and history.

Nevertheless, both of my grandfathers had a similar and strong motivation to leave their homeland and migrate to America.

They were very courageous to leave their birthplace homes, even though the life must have been very difficult there.

How they got the money and made the difficult exit and passage arrangements is unknown. Neither had known any friends who immigrated to the United States.

But all of us are so thankful that they did persevere or else we would have had to live through the maelstrom of Europe in the 1930's and '40's. Of course, we wouldn't have been us.

Benjamin L. Jaffe, my fraternal grandfather, brought his wife and Henry, his infant son of six months, to New York in 1889. Sarah, his wife, was a tiny woman who ultimately gave birth to seven children. She was an Orthodox Jewish woman, typical of that time, whose entire interest in life was caring for and performing the extensive housework for a large family, and practicing her religion. Benjamin became a founder and trustee of the prominent Fifth Street Synagogue in Washington, D. C., where they moved to shortly after arriving in America. He made a living as a housepainter, and the business grew large and prosperous and eventually employed his three sons and over 50 painters and paperhangers. The eldest, Henry, married Mildred Loewenberg, and they were my parents.

Sigmund Loewenberg, my other grandfather, was typically proud of his German-Jewish ancestry, and settled in Newark, N. J. He married Bertha Cohn who was born in Warrenton, Virginia, of all places. How and why she got there is not known, but it is probable that her father was an itinerant merchant selling some wares off of a horse and wagon. Virginia was very appealing to him and he set up shop there and prospered.

Sigmund Loewenberg owned and ran a small sporting goods manufacturing business. They manufactured golf bags, hunting jackets and rifle cases. The factory, located in downtown Newark, New Jersey, was a relic of an industry popular during World War I. It made a generous amount of clothing and equipment for that war.

Visiting the factory in the early 30's, I was impressed by the extensive product line, but disappointed with the equipment. The elevator for the four-story operation had its cage fronted by a gate of wooden rods, which was raised and lowered by hand. At that age I thought that using an elevator with some manual dexterity was fun. I never realized it was entirely outdated. The manufacturing equipment was equally antiquated. Grandpa eventually sold the business on a fair basis to a competitor.

The painting and decorating business became the most prominent in Washington. Among its customers were many government buildings and the White House, then the residence of Calvin Coolidge, President of the United States. The New York Decorating Co., as it was named, expanded into house renovation and construction and built a number of projects such as an 88-house development in Alexandria, Virginia.

The streets in Washington D.C. were laid out in a grid by L'Enfante, the Revolutionary War hero, a friend of George Washington and an ally from France. The first set of streets running east and west from the Capitol were named by letters of the alphabet such as E Street or M Street. Next, going north, streets were named with one syllable in alphabetic order such as in Park Road. In the same alphabetic sequence, eventually streets were named with two syllables as in Euclid Street, followed by streets with three syllables such as Allison Street, the first street in the fourth alphabet. At the time we moved there, very little was north of the fourth alphabet. This condition was later changed by frantic construction and development.

Life on Fifteenth Street was mostly pleasant. The north-south streets were numbered and the avenues, which so many people found confusing, were diagonal and named after states. There were the usual childhood problems, relations with peers, arguments with parents and playtime activities, coupled with delivering newspapers, and selling subscriptions to magazines. We rolled Easter eggs on the White House lawn and shook hands with the President.

My very first recollection was of the 1924 eclipse. We watched it from the tiny terrace of our apartment on Columbia Road, NW, in Washington and I wondered if I would see it every few years. That was about the same time that I acquired my first scar—a one-stitch job between my eyebrows when I used my parent's double bed as a trampoline and fell, hitting my head on the wooden headboard. I eventually ended up with over 30 stitches during the following 80 years.

We had moved there from what was my family's first residence—on New Hampshire Avenue near 17th Street Northwest.

In the next block was a delicatessen where, I remember, there was a glass fronted wooden cabinet on a table with an opening at the bottom where crisp, delicious potato chips settled down to be scooped up and put in a brown paper bag. I tastily remember the bottom tray and grabbing those always crisp and delicious chips. There were also mouth-watering pickles in a barrel. Not many pre-packaged things in those days. Today Americans eat 31% more packaged food than fresh food.*

From Columbia Road, the most noteworthy remembrance was being taken to the grand opening of a small park at Columbia Road and 16th Street containing a statue of a Civil war general rampant on horseback. My folks could afford a part-time nurse then, and she took me to the event. A band played marches and the statue was unveiled, accompanied by sparklers. It was an impressionable day.

When I was just six years old, we moved to what was to be our primary residence at 4423 15th St. NW, at the corner of Allison Street.

I walked to grade school. It was roughly a mile to my grade school and eventually to my junior high and high school. We never had the luxury of school buses in those days. Quite intuitively, with Frank Rich, Sylvan Stein and Dick Cash, with whom I walked to

---

*N.Y. Times—April 4, 2010

school every day, we rented a vacant store on 14th St. and sold boxes of candy at retail during holidays.

My parents, Mildred and Henry, divorced in 1935 and the lawyer demanded that I leave camp three weeks early to be in Washington at that time. This was a real shock to me. I loved camp and reveled in all the activities.

For many years I had had the good fortune to be sent to a summer camp in Maine. The camp was called Indian Acres. I loved the sports activities and although I was never superlative in any one of them, I won gold medals in each sport for many years—the most gold medals ever won by anyone up to that time. Eventually I became a junior counselor and tennis counselor. The latter probably happened, not because I was such a great tennis player or such a wonderful teacher, but because it didn't cost too much to pay me for this service.

When my parents divorced, Dad left home. In those days it was much more of a stigma and made life more difficult for me and my brother Kenneth and sister Marjorie. However as the saying goes, "If it doesn't kill you, it only makes you stronger."

Irwin Jaffe—1929—Age 9

L-R: Kenneth Jaffe, Marjorie Jaffe, Irwin Jaffe—1934

Camp Indian Acres, Tennis Counselor—1939

The White House, Washington, D.C.—1930
Henry Jaffe, center front

Mildred and Henry Jaffe—1930

The DEALER'S
50-YEAR CLUB

•

Sigmund Loewenberg, Ordered to Take Life Easy, Stays Active as Goodwill Ambassador for Hughes

SIGMUND LOEWENBERG

NEXT month Sigmund Loewenberg will celebrate his fiftieth year in the sporting goods industry. Formerly o w n e r of the Loewenberg Company, Newark, N. J., and more recently identified with Hughes Consolidated, Inc., New York City, successor to the original firm, Loewenberg continues to call on his friends in the trade, lugging samples and chatting about sporting goods.

Back in 1883, at the New York 'bor, the SS Fulda steamed up the bay to its berth at Hoboken. Aboard was Sigmund Loewenberg. He was spellbound by the sight of the Brooklyn Bridge, because the modest town from which he hailed had nothing in comparison.

The first hotel Loewenberg stopped at was at Broadway and Prince street. He reached there by stage coach.

Ten years later, in 1893, Loewenberg set up his own business at 285 Bank street, Newark, N. J., as a custom tailor, making automobile dusters and butchers' aprons.

In 1898, there was an opportunity to get into the hunting clothing business through an arrangement with Richard Hill at Boyden Place. Hill knew the styles of outdoor apparel and how to produce an attractive line. Hill and Loewenberg worked together, but in a few years Hill died and Loewenberg expanded the hunting apparel line by himself.

A similar opportunity, in 1912, presented itself in regard to golf bags. That was also the year the firm moved to 58 Colden street, Newark, the present factory address of Hughes Consolidated, Inc. The first bags were round, stayless affairs with a single ball pocket fastened by strap and buckle.

The firm was growing nicely. Loewenberg saw his business expand from a modest house with three operators to a concern with a staff of 50 employes in 1918. Part of the growth was due to the orders which poured into the plant during World War I, calling for canvas leggings and mackinaws.

Loewenberg recalled some of his original customers and without hesitation mentioned Alex Taylor & Company, Solomon's of Elizabeth, N. J., Vaughan of Paterson, N. J., Da vega, Harry C. Lee and the former Schoverling, Daly & Gales and Thomas Conroy.

In the late '30s, doctors suggested that Loewenberg take things easy and shift his responsibilities to others. On January 1, 1938, the assets, stocks and machinery of the company were taken over by Hughes Consolidated, Inc., with Edwin J. Hughes as president and Louis Salzburg, plant manager, as vice-president. Loewenberg is not a stockholder in the new firm, but acts as a goodwill ambassador between the factory and the dealers. In some cases there are three generations of workers employed at the 58 Colden street plant, thus preserving for the new firm the Loewenberg quality and tradition by inheritance. Plant enlargement and improved facilities took place at the change.

BUTCHERS' APRONS AND AUTO DUSTERS were made in Sigmund Loewenberg's first store at 285 Bank street, Newark, N. J. That's Loewenberg in the center, winking.

L-R: Mildred, Irwin, Bertha Lowenberg (Grandmother)
and Great-Grandfather Loewenberg

Bertha and Sigmund Loewenberg—Grandparents

Benjamin Jaffe—Grandparent

L-R: Henry Jaffe, Benjamin Jaffe, Harry Jaffe, Morris Jaffe

CHAPTER 4

SHIPWRECK

> **H.M.M.V. Southern Prince**
> **Hudson River Pier**
> **45th Street**
> **Manhattan, NY**
> **June 8, 1937**

His Majesty's Motor Vessel was at the dock on the Hudson River, impatiently awaiting passengers and crew. It was a small 10,000-ton ship with comfortable accommodations for 100 passengers as well as freight. Its itinerary provided stops at Rio de Janeiro and Santos, Brazil, Montevideo, Uruguay before turning around at Buenos Aires, Argentina. I signed on as a Bellhop for the trip to South America and return. I did not need a passport as my working papers fulfilled that function as well as stipulating that my employment was for six months and I had to be returned to New York City for termination. There was, however a verbal understanding with the Furness Prince Line, owner of the vessel, that I was only signed for the six week round trip.

This was the first time I was alone in New York—or anywhere—more than 50 miles from Washington. It was exciting. In the evening, I walked the six long blocks from the dock to Broadway. Famous Broadway! I discovered the Automat, a quirky restaurant germane to New York where the food was offered in little cubicles with glass doors which could be opened by putting a coin, usually a quarter, in the slot. I also devoured all the exciting, entertaining activities which Broadway offered.

After two days the ship departed.

It was an English ship and the crew was mostly English. Unlike American ships, the crew was not unionized.

On this ship in 1937 the steward crew, of which I was a member, ate all of their meals standing up at a small rectangular table which had room for only about one-quarter of the crew at a time. That wasn't so good, but the food was the same as served to the passengers, which was very good.

My berth was in a room below decks with a dozen other sailors. Although most of the crew was what you might consider as tough guys, fortunately, I got along with them very well.

The first stop was glamorous, exciting Rio, with famous Copacabana beach and loads of attractive, sensuous girls. In my youth, I had never been around femmes fatales who could sing and dance like professionals, then give you a wink that made your body shake and quiver. But I was to get no closer to them than a wistful look over the ship's rail at the dock. My boss was the Second Officer of the ship in charge of the steward crew. He revoked my shore privilege because of some perceived failing in my work. This was certainly a bitter disappointment to me.

The next stop was Santos, slightly south of Rio. It was there that I literally went up in the air. Happy Day!

The airplane runway was a sandy beach and I can still remember that flight as if it were yesterday. It was my very first airplane flight. It was exhilarating! In the evening we did what sailors usually do. We went to a local "house of entertainment."

Shortly before I had left Washington, Rose, my sweet, selfless, maiden aunt took me to her Clinic where she worked as a registered nurse. Its main treatment was to cure venereal disease and I got a frightening view of the various stages of the cases. My other maiden aunt, Bessie, was the traveler and she was the one who arranged for the prized bellhop job for me through her friend Mr. Fazachaly, the Scotchman who was the chief purser on the ship.

The pleasure palace was a neat and clean residence. It was furnished with an assortment of attractive traditional sofas, chairs, and tables. The lamps emanated a warm light throughout the second floor reception room. It was populated by six attractive, sparsely clad young ladies who immediately selected a sailor to sit next to and serve a drink. The young lady who selected me was just a girl, only slightly older than I. Nevertheless we got very close, and she finally whispered into my ear, "Fuckee, fuckee, fuckee." I was enjoying the Brazilian beer, comfortably relaxed, and finding new ways to enjoy this girl who threw off vibrations of exciting sex. However, I also could not erase from my mind the ugly scenes of the results of venereal disease which I saw so dramatically in the clinic in Washington. This captured my sixteen year old reasoning and I left Santos as chaste as I entered. I always debated whether I should thank Aunt Rose.

I never sent many letters home during the summer but the following one was one of the few.

Dear Folks,

I was half-sitting, half-lying on the cargo hatch watching the smoke from my cigarette describe vague patterns in the night, when the thought struck me. Indeed, this was an unusual sight. H.M.M.V. "Southern Prince" was leisurely plowing through the calm sea on her regular run from New York to South America. At once my interest was aroused, and I immediately devoured the scene, lest the magnificence of it should suddenly be broken.

The hatch on which I was lounging was situated on the after deck. Directly forward was the passenger's section, the cabins being on the same level, and the swimming pool and lounge one deck higher.

I listened. Somewhere below, the crew was singing. The tune drifted slowly through the hatches and filled the night around me. I flipped my cigarette over the rail, and it described a graceful arc, glowing brightly in its last moment of glory before it was extinguished by the waves. Another sound came to me—the passengers. They too figured in this rare scene. The distant hum of their voices, punctuated by the throb-throb-throb of the gallant ship calmly gliding through the waves.

As I looked overhead, I sensed that what I saw would be fully in accord with the prevalent scene. I was not mistaken, for the myriads of stars seemed all to be winking at me through the cloudless infinity between us. Off to the left, the huge yellow sphere that was the moon just rising from the depths of the ocean, its warm glow leisurely dropping to the surface of the water to come shimmering over the waves and pat against the hull of the ship.

Astern, the propellers cut through the water, leaving behind a wake that gradually died down to hundreds of tiny whirlpools, all hammering against each other in a struggle for existence. From the sides came the soft pat-pat-slap of the waves gently breaking against the side. I took a deep breath and smelled the sharp tang of the salt air about me.

This was all so peaceful and restful—the ship, the stars, the moon and the water. All the atmosphere seemed to be in union, and I slipped off into the most peaceful element of all—sleep.

Love to all,

Irwin*

Heading south to Montevideo, the Southern Prince logged routine days. The weather was good and the seas calm. My work station was standing on the main deck at the central stairwell. The other bellboy and I split the day and early evening duty hours. Actually there were not many calls.

The worst part of this job was the boredom caused by lack of work. We reached Montevideo in the afternoon exactly on schedule, and the rest of the day my fellow bellboy and I went ashore and took a tour of the city. Montevideo was a very different foreign country. The people were friendly and there were many interesting sights. But there really was nothing terribly noteworthy.

The next day the ship left for Buenos Aires. To get there we had to traverse the Rio de la Plata, a very wide, very shallow river mouth. Montevideo was on the northern bank of the river and Buenos Aires on the south bank and further west.

I was off duty and sleeping. This, in itself, was not unusual for me. At about 3:00 p.m. in the afternoon someone shook me awake. "Hurry, get the hell outa here. We've been hit by another boat and we're sinking." I rushed topside. The passengers and crew were forming orderly groups wearing life jackets. A large freighter was back-

---

*In college Irwin became Jaff which ultimately ended up as Jeff.

23

ing slowly away from a gashing hole it had made in our portside amidships. A portion of the hole was below the water line and water was rushing into the lower decks. Slowly the Southern Prince, its engines stopped, drifted to what was the side of a channel which ran through the very shallow river mouth. The ship was sinking and listing to its side at about a 15 degree angle. Finally it came to an abrupt stop and fortunately rested outside the channel in forty feet of water. This was close to the exact spot that the Nazi super battleship GRAF SPEE was cornered and sunk during World War II.

An Argentine Coast Guard boat soon arrived and all of the passengers were easily taken aboard for what was the unexpected and undesired final leg of their trip to Buenos Aires. There was little excitement. It was as if this was a routine disembarkment in port.

The crew was required to stay aboard because, if the ship was abandoned, it could have been salvaged by anyone. We could not use our regular quarters for the five days we remained there, as they were underwater. We slept in blankets in the main dining room and ate there on the sloping deck. We took turns playing records from a salvaged record player. I managed to find one with Dick Powell singing "Shipmates stand together. Don't give up the ship." It was a song from one of his movies. It did not make a great hit with the crew.

A concrete slab was fitted into the damaged hull, the water pumped out and we were towed to our dock in Buenos Aires.

For nearly six weeks, I was a happy captive in Buenos Aires. My daily work consisted of scraping, painting railings, cleaning, running errands and miscellaneous ship's work.

Each evening we were free and several times a week we enjoyed three course dinners of magnificent Argentine beef with a string quartet playing beautiful classical music, all for $2.00.* Even so it

---

*$29.78 in 2009 dollars—AIER

was only possible by steady remittances of father's cash via Western Union. My pay as a bellboy was $5.00 per week. I had a great opportunity to satisfy a tourist's view of a wonderful city and a poignantly different culture.

Inasmuch as Furness was not required to disembark me in New York for six months, this met with great disfavor with my family. They could not stand the thought of my missing any school days. Dad sent me a ticket to be a passenger on an American ship going to New York. The trip turned out to be a great delight, full of fun for me as probably the youngest and most curious passenger. The most noteworthy incident was the news of the tragic loss of Amelia Earhart somewhere in the Pacific.

My plan to save him a lot of money by not going to summer camp didn't exactly work out.

I didn't have a passport so Dad had to go to the State Department and get special permission for me to enter the U.S. Then he had to ride out to the ship in New York harbor on the pilot's boat and give me the papers.

We all had an interesting summer.

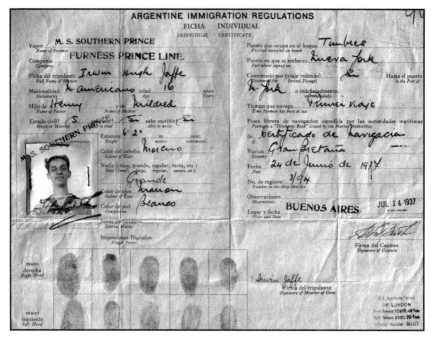

Argentine Immigration Form

Certificate of Discharge

WASHINGTON HERALD-TIMES.—Washington

Home Newspaper—SUNDAY, SEPTEMBER 26, 1937

Telephone District 5260-5275

D. C. Boy, 16, Proves Hero in Shipwreck

Irwin Jaffe Returns Home Safe After Near-Tragic Experience

Irwin Jaffe, 16-year-old Washington boy, went down to the sea in a ship, and darn' near stayed down.

But Irwin was back home yesterday none the worse for his near-tragic experience, ready to resume his studies at the Devitt School for Boys on Connecticut Ave., with a nautical tale to tell that would curl your hair—the story of how, as a cabin boy, he stuck by the liner Southern Prince when the ship, with 27 feet of water sloshing in her hold, was settling on a Uruguayan mud bank.

Five Days There

For five days, Irwin tells you, his eyes shining with the memory of his first seagoing adventure, the crew stayed aboard the Southern Prince in a lonely mud-lined channel of the Rio de la Plata, with no radio, and home 8,000 miles away.

Adventure? There had already been plenty of it, in a mild way, Irwin says, since the day when he decided to go to sea for the summer as a cabin boy. But there was almost too much when a freighter rammed the Southern Prince in mid-channel, turned cabins into a jumble of twisted steel, and opened the liner's plates like the sides of a wet cardboard box.

Mystery Wreck

"The wreck was a complete mystery to all the crew," Irwin said. "I was asleep in my cabin taking an afternoon nap when I heard a terrific jarring and crashing, and the ship lurched. I threw on some clothes and went on deck.

"I could hardly believe it at first when they told me there'd been a wreck, but then I saw the freighter backing off with her prow smashed.

"The ship's log said it was a foggy day afterward, I was told, but I didn't have much time to look, because the crew went right to work to get the passengers off."

They unloaded 32 passengers in 30 minutes, Irwin said, assisted by a coast patrol boat that was standing by.

Some of the crew left the found-

IRWIN JAFFE
Adventure a-Plenty

ering liner, he added, but with several others, he remained aboard to clear up some of the debris from the wreck.

The Southern Prince was finally patched up temporarily and towed into Buenos Aires, whence Jaffe took passage for New York aboard the Munson liner Southern Cross — returning, for a change, as a first class passenger.

At quarantine in New York harbor, he ran into the last hazard of a tough trip, he said—the State Department didn't want to let him come 'home, because as a sailor on a British-owned vessel, he had no passport.

Met by Father

But his father, Henry Jaffe, interior decorator who lives at 911 Thirteenth St. N. W., had anticipated that difficulty, and met him with a State Department pass.

Irwin, who graduated from Roosevelt High School last June, said the only person injured in the collision was a passenger who cut his finger when he was thrown from his demolished bunk.

CHAPTER 5

GETTING THROUGH SCHOOL

> **Virginia Polytechnic Institute**
> **Blacksburg, VA**
> **Sept. 1939**

At Virginia Tech I was a cadet in the ROTC program. Coupled with my three years in the Washington D.C. Roosevelt High School cadet corps, I had seven years of experience and easily accepted discipline, military organization, personal and group responsibility, as well as maintaining those leadership traits I had learned so many years ago. These were important factors in my development. Even though it was a big personal disappointment to never achieve a rank above sergeant in either school or in the army, I was nevertheless the lead sergeant when the Roosevelt regiment won the citywide drill competition. A bad first step or faulty cadence would have been a disaster.

In as much as I skipped three half grades in grammar school, my parents decided to send me to the Devitt Prep School in Washington for a year, so I would be more mature when I started college.

As a freshman in college I was selected to be on my G company drill team which won that prestigious competition in 1939. I proudly was one of the few to wear the "1" patch on my uniform sleeve. Many years later I was equally proud to sponsor the "Jaffe Eager Squad Drill Competition" at Virginia Tech with cash prizes for the annual winners. The Commandant of Cadets lauded this as an important motivating activity for the Cadet Corps in perpetuity.

I studied Architectural Engineering. I knew I was only a mediocre student. It was not that the work was too difficult, it was actually easy. It was rather that I found other things of greater interest. I was on the basketball team which took lots of my time, although I was not a starter. I was Editor-in-Chief of the college newspaper, The Virginia Tech. In addition, I became the Business Manager of the VPI Directory and Associate Editor of the Virginia Tech Engineer Magazine. Where could I find the time to study architecture? I was invited to join three honorary fraternities. At Virginia Tech, there were no social fraternities. The three honorary fraternities were ODK—Leadership; Pi Delta Epsilon—Publications; and Alpha Psi Omega—dramatics.

At that time Virginia Tech had another program. It was known by the initials CPTP. It stood for the Civilian Pilots Training Program.

The training airplanes were Fleet-Model I bi-planes, old World War I, open dual cockpits with 125 h.p. engines. That was enough power to take off - barely. The class of eight wore cotton helmets and goggles and considered themselves a squadron of fighter pilots. In 1939, with such overtones of German aggression, becoming a pilot was a serious matter. Learning to fly in a Fleet was simple. There was an air speed indicator, an altimeter, a fuel gauge, rudder pedals and a joystick, which worked the ailerons. In those days starting the engine was accomplished by having someone spin the propeller by hand. One of the training flights included practicing tailspins and recovery. It was only a few years before that tailspins were considered fatal. That stopped when the great Jimmie Doolittle, who was to become famous for the aircraft carrier sortie bombing of Japan, accidentally got into a tailspin. Feeling fatalistic, he decided to hurry his crash and pushed the joystick straight down. That and a kick of the rudder pedals stopped the spinning and allowed him to slowly pull the stick back, bring the plane to level flight and land safely.

On this flight as we lifted the nose of the plane higher and higher until it stalled and the nose dropped into a roller-coaster, breath-taking dive and began to spin, my instructor, Al Preissner yelled into the voice tube (non-electric) that his stick wasn't working—must have a broken cable. He calmly talked me into the actions that would take us out of the spin. I, not quite so calmly, followed his instructions and we landed safely with me at the controls.

Flying solo, especially cross-country, was to say the least, incredibly exhilarating. It was a new view, a new world. It was all the more exciting because it all depended on me. There was no one to help if something happened, and being in control was adrenaline pounding. It was an experience never to be forgotten.

I was very proud of my Pilot's License.

In 1939 when I entered Virginia Tech, and became a freshman in the Corps of Cadets, the "RAT SYSTEM" was a base of the training program. Freshmen were constantly harried by upperclassmen. There were many requirements.

When walking anywhere on campus, Rats were required to assume a "brace." This consisted of chin tucked down to chest, shoulders pushed back, all in an exaggerated vertical position, arms moving in a marching motion. "Square meals" were required at the dining room table where the upper classmen never missed an opportunity to chastise the Rats if they did not lift the food-laden fork exactly in a vertical path and then a right angle to the mouth and return in the same way. Physical abuse was limited to things like being forced to squat and hold a rifle straight out at arms length.

The system was used for many years, but is now called the "New Cadet Training Program" and some things like "square meals" were discontinued but the new cadets still have to sit on the front 3" of their chair.

The system was designed to develop personal discipline. You have to learn how to follow before you can lead. It works! Virginia Tech, along with several other ROTC institutions, has an enviable record of developing successful leaders for both military and civilian life.

While at Tech I met John Elder who was in the class one year ahead of me. John grew up on a farm in Virginia. I got to know him when I began working on the Virginia Tech college newspaper and he became my mentor. He was modest and soft-spoken. He was my predecessor as Editor-in-Chief and invited me to join him on a trip to Washington, D.C. for a convention of college newspaper personnel. While there, he met the lovely Jane, who ultimately became his wife. We all became very warm friends.

John, the country boy, was brilliant. There was no doubt about it. His career included being the head of the U.S. Army Engineers in Vietnam, and a member of the Joint Chiefs of Staff at the Pentagon in Washington, D.C. where I visited him. He was a General and was head of PLANNING, usually assigned to the brightest person available. He was offered a promotion to be Commanding General of NATO but retired instead and served as a consultant to the armed services for many years. He was a mentor to Brent Scowcroft who became the National Security Advisor to Presidents Ford and the senior George Bush.

It was a sad privilege for me to be with his family at his funeral in Arlington National Cemetery. He was accorded a full military ceremony with marching troops, rifle salute and a horse drawn caisson. It was a fitting farewell to a great, but unsung, American Patriot.

At Virginia Tech the leadership training, which I received in the Corp of Cadets provided a most solid base for what was so important in all of my future activities.

ROOSEVELT HIGH CADETS CAPTURE HONORS—The Fifth Regiment was awarded first place in the regimental drill held at Central High School Stadium. Company L is shown on parade above. Below, Dr. Harvey A. Smith, assistant superintendent of schools, presenting a gold medal to the officers of the regiment. From left—Lieut. Col. George Christy, Capt. Marshall Ratter, Sergt. Irwin Jaffe and Dr. Smith.

Regimental Winners—1937

THE VIRGINIA TECH

"AMERICA'S MOST MODERN COLLEGIATE NEWSPAPER"

VOL. XXXVIII, No. 23   VIRGINIA POLYTECHNIC INSTITUTE, BLACKSBURG, VIRGINIA, APRIL 3, 1941   Price Ten Cents

Publication Heads for '42 Picked

Jaffe, Branum to be Tech Ed., Bus. Mgr.

New heads for the various publications were selected last Tuesday, and announced at a banquet held that night by the Publications Board. The elections were held in the Tech office, and detailed papers presented by the candidates outlining experiences in publication work, personal data, and proposed policy, were carefully considered before final selections were made.

The new staff of The Virginia Tech is headed by I. H. Jaffe as editor-in-chief, P. Bontecou as managing editor, and C. F. Branum as business manager. J. L. Lankford and E. W. Christ received the posts in The Tech Engineer elections as editor and business manager, respectively. R. N. Bo-

dine and N. S. Sharp were named to be editor and business manager of The 1942 Bugle. The Sentinel, recently authorized as an official Tech publication, will have D. Shotton filling the post of managing editor.

"Jeff" Jaffe hails from Washington, D. C., and has had three years of experience on the Tech editorial staff. A cadet in G Company, he is also a member of the Maroon Mask Honor Society, and has been advertising manager for the dramatic group for the past two years. He is enrolled in architectural engineering, and has also worked on the Tech Engineer for three years. Pierre Bontecou, corporal from I Battery, is from Hopewell. Also a member of the Tech staff for three years, he belongs to the Piedmont Club and is chairman of the Junior Ring Dance Publicity Committee. "Brains" Branum, O Battery, calls Harrisonburg his home. He is a member of The Order of De-Molay, the AIEE, and has also worked with the Tech for three years.

Jack Lankford, N Battery corporal, is a Yankee from Forest Hills, N. Y. A member of the ASME, he has worked a year and a half on the Engineer, and has evidenced

IRWIN HUGH JAFFE
Washington, D. C.

Architectural Engineering
Engineer

Co. G (1, 2, 3, 4), Pfc. (2), Corp. (3).
Freshman Basketball.
Freshman Baseball.
Intramural Sports (1, 2, 3, 4).
Omicron Delta Kappa (3), Corresponding Secretary (4).
Pi Delta Epsilon (3), Historian (4).
Maroon Mask Honor Society (2, 3, 4).
Alpha Psi Omega, Cast Director (4).
The Virginia Tech (1, 2, 3, 4), Desk Editor (3), Editor-in-Chief (4).
The Virginia Tech Engineer (1, 2, 3), Associate Editor (4).
BUGLE (1).
V. P. I. Directory, Business Manager (4).
Architectural Club (1, 2).
American Institute of Architects (3, 4).
Capitol Club (1, 2, 3, 4).
Maroon Mask (1, 2, 3, 4), Business Manager (3).

"Jeff"

53

Virginia Tech Yearbook—1942

Camp Indian Acres—1938

CHAPTER 6

THIS WAS MY WAR

Ft. Belvoir, VA
September 1943
World War II

I spent part of the summer between my junior and senior years at Tech in the local hospital with pneumonia which I caught when several of us spent a rainy afternoon trying to get a small plane, which crash landed in a cornfield, back to the airport. This meant that I missed the ROTC summer camp requirement to become a lieutenant in the United States Army which had always been my fervent desire. I also missed enough school credits so that I was not able to graduate with my class of 1942. I had to miss my college graduation ceremony. Nevertheless, same as high school, I did graduate and receive my diploma from both institutions.

To make up for the missed summer ROTC camp I had to attend Officer Candidate School after graduation in 1943. This was at the Army Engineer Corps' facility at Fort Belvoir, Virginia. I had majored in Architectural Engineering at Tech.

I spent several weeks undergoing some of the toughest physical and mental work, not to even mention those unforgiving first sergeants who would constantly keep us on our toes. I was called in for a routine physical exam. Two days later my Captain told me that I was released from the Army because of physical disability. The problem was Osteosclerosis fragilis, a slight hyper-calcification of my bones which might have a tendency to break easily. I was surprised because just the other day we had practiced running full speed with our rifle and back pack and throwing ourselves to the ground as if under enemy fire. No broken bones.

I refused to accept this.

I contacted medical specialists to prove that I was physically able to serve. I applied to the Navy, the Marines and to the Ambulance Corps. No one would accept me. This discharge probably saved my life as I would have served in the high casualty rate Engineer Corps.

I had no choice but to return to civilian life. It wasn't so bad except for the psychological trauma of being a 4-F and not being able to do my share in the war for which all Americans, regardless of age, gender or race strongly favored.

I returned to the painting, decorating and construction business.

I have always felt guilty about my inability to have served my country in World War II.

HEADQUARTERS
THE ENGINEER SCHOOL
FORT BELVOIR, VIRGINIA

May 17, 1943

ORDERS)

117)

$\underline{E X T R A C T}$

* * * *

7. ROTC graduate <u>Irwin Hugh Jaffe</u>, Co S, 3rd Engr Sch Regt,
her attendance at the Engr Officer Candidate School, this sta, eff
3, and will be returned to his home at: 4423 15th St. NW, Washing
Auth: Ltr TAGO AG 201-Jaffe, Irwin Hugh, (3-19-43) PR-A, A & I.
ay 5, 1943. In lieu of T and Subs while traveling the FD will pay
r' 5¢ per mile. As an alternative to Auth travel alws TO will furn
reimb him for the actual cost of meals at not to exceed $3.00 per
uth: Par 3 AR 35-3520. TDN. TO will furn T SOS 3 P 520-02 A 1605

* * * *

By Order of Colonel PRICE:

G. R. HULL

CHAPTER 7

HENRY AND BERT

**April 1945
Canal Street
Manhattan, NY**

After graduating from the Virginia Polytechnic Institute, I worked in the painting and construction business, but soon realized that while I liked the business, I didn't want to work in a business where my two uncles outvoted my father. More important, I felt that there were many more interesting and productive activities on which to build a career. I left for New York City in April 1945, and sublet a small apartment in Brooklyn. Each morning I would ride into Manhattan with my friend, Cy Cutler, and begin work at my "office"—the third phone booth from the front in a Whelan drug store on Canal Street. My work consisted of looking for a job, which I eventually found with an interior designer as a construction supervisor. My education as an architectural engineer, and my construction experience stood me in good stead and work progressed very nicely. However, I was asked to work on a particular Saturday, not unusual for that job. I had tickets for myself and my intended wife for just that Saturday to attend the Harvard-Yale football game. This was something we did not want to miss. I claimed I was sick. Unfortunately my boss found out that I wasn't really sick that day and I was summarily fired.

As I looked for another job, my new father-in-law managed to find me a position with a food broker as a missionary man selling to retail grocers. About six months later, I obtained a job in the factory of the Loft Candy Co. in Queens, New York. This was hard physical work which was mostly lifting, pouring, and mixing various ingredients used to make the many candy products which Loft offered for sale in its retail stores. While it was never intended that I would become a candymaker, it served as a solid background for the candy business.

Both my father Henry, and my father-in-law, Bert, died very young. Their ages were 62 and 55 respectively.

I had great respect and affection for both and deeply regretted this loss. They were successful businessmen and I learned a lot from each about business and life.

One of the most important things I learned from them was integrity. There were no lectures, no discussions, nor was it ever verbalized. But I saw and heard both of them always keeping to the difficult path of integrity, including integrity of deed and integrity of thought. Their quiet example was strong and compelling and never flaunted.

Whenever you are to do a thing
though it can never be known but to yourself,
ask yourself how you would act were
the whole world looking at you, and act accordingly.

—Thomas Jefferson

Henry was cold, smart and tough but was always ready to help. He always tried to "fill the holes in front of you before you stepped in them." Cooperation and "always walk fast" were important characteristics which I acquired from him.

Bert was warm, smart and tough and also ready to help. He was an excellent businessman and earned great respect from everyone with whom he came in contact. From him I learned to "get it done." I was proud to have him as my father-in-law.

I was then given a position as a clerk in the advertising department of the Tootsie Roll Company which Bert Rubin owned with his family. I ultimately became Advertising Manager. We enjoyed each other's company and were equally elated as the company grew. Then, without warning, Bert Rubin died. At that time Bert's brother, Bill, who with their father shared a trust for the ownership of the company, took over as President. For over six months after he took over the presidency, Bill never spoke to me. He never asked me about my work and never assigned me any activities. He also never had the guts to fire me.

I decided to leave the company and found a bankrupt candy company in which I was able to buy a 50% interest.

We are all faced with a series of great opportunities—
brilliantly disguised as insoluble problems.

—John W. Gardner

Henry Jaffe

Bert Rubin

CHAPTER 8

RECOVERY ON DELANCEY STREET

February 10, 1950
Delancey Street, Manhattan
New York, NY

I t was a cold and windy day when I walked down Delancey Street in the lower East Side of Manhattan. I shivered a little and not just from the cold. I was about to enter the office of the Chunky Chocolate Co. for the first time and meet my new partner, Phil Silvershein.

Almost no one knows that Delancey Street was named after a French nobleman who was a great ally and supporter of George Washington during the American Revolution. But over the decades, the street was not inhabited by people of French ancestries. Rather it had become a flowering center for Eastern European Jews who immigrated to America in the late 1800's.

The street boasted several famous restaurants, one of which— Ratner's—was a dairy restaurant where the busy, patronizing waiters would usually whisk your saucer away when you lifted your cup to sip the coffee.

If you walked down Delancey Street in the mid-forties and fifties as it approached the Williamsburg Bridge, both sides of the street were lined with a myriad assortment of ethnic shops. The one exception was a Woolworth 5-&-10-cent store neatly situated right in the center of everything.

During my early days as a fifty-percent partner in the new candy business, I could hear a constant hum of traffic proceeding onto and off of the Williamsburg bridge. The original CHUNKY factory was near the eastern end of the street as it lifted itself gradually onto the bridge. It was at the intersection of Ridge Street which, filling the dual purpose of receiving and shipping platform, was often blocked when trucks were delivering the materials needed or shipping out the finished products.

I had just bought a 50% interest in a bankrupt business. I hadn't any money of my own, and it was the kindness and confidence my mother-in-law held for me that caused her to lend me the $25,000* which it cost. She was a gentle, caring woman who had been widowed from Bert Rubin, the Chairman and CEO of Tootsie Rolls until his death a few years before.

She had confidence in me, going back to the days when I first became a part of the family by marrying her daughter, Natalie. Behind every successful man stands a surprised mother-in-law. Her husband, Bert Rubin, a genial, successful and well-respected man had taken control of the Sweets Co. of America, makers of Tootsie Rolls in 1935. It was then a tiny operation with a factory in Hell's Kitchen area of Manhattan—11th Ave. and 38th St.

---

*$222,400 in 2009 dollars—A.I.E.R.

Although Sweets Co. was a public company and listed on the New York Stock Exchange, there was no such thing as a tender offer for stock in those days. So Bert, with the help and advice provided by a banker Mr. Lewis Clark, traveled around the country, meeting with the various stockholders and buying their stock. They were happy to accept a low but fair offer for the stock as the company paid no dividend and had languished sleepily for years. They saw no future for Tootsie Rolls.

But Bert Rubin did!

He was able to get control of the company with his father, Joseph Rubin, and his brother, Bill. Neither Joseph or Bill ever worked at Tootsie Rolls and Bert built it up to be a substantial entity in the confectionery industry. This engendered a bitter jealousy on the part of Bill who was limited to running the family folding box business—a supplier of boxes to Tootsie Rolls, which is where Bert got the idea of trying to acquire the company. He had built the business from a tiny operation to a position of prominence in the candy industry, and unfortunately passed away in 1948 at a relatively young age. He was well loved by friends, family and business associates and even competitors. There were over 1500 people who attended his funeral.

When I married Natalie I was working for an industrial designer in New York City. I had left my family's decorating and construction business in Washington, D. C. I knew that life could be more exciting and more productive somewhere else. New York seemed to beckon me. So I crossed my fingers and took the big step. I met Natalie Rubin on a blind date and after six months we were married. My father-in-law, probably fearing that his daughter might starve being married to me, was kind enough to offer me a job with Tootsie Rolls. It only took one minute of careful consideration before I accepted.

That acceptance was my entry into my lifelong love of the candy industry.

The business, of which I now owned half, was housed in a small, two story brick building on the corner of Ridge and Delancey Streets in downtown Manhattan. The factory was on the first floor, and had one room on the second floor, the rest of which was rented to another small candy factory. There were no sales people, no office personnel, and only 4 workmen in the "factory."

Well it wasn't much of a business. It had thrived during World War II because it had good sugar and chocolate quotas and the owner, Silvershein, was able to sell all of the CHUNKYS he could make without any sales or marketing costs. After the war he turned the business over to his eldest son, who, unwisely, tried to run the business in the same rather arrogant manner in which they were able to operate during the war shortages.

It was clearly predictable that after the war the wholesale customers and the retailers would not tolerate such high-handed actions, and the business soon went bankrupt.

Phil, the father, bought the business back from the New York Creditmen's Association, which had acquired the company when it went under. He not only needed money to run the business, but he needed someone younger who could handle the myriad of day-to-day affairs in running the business, especially now that he was getting on in years. His original business was as a candy wholesaler in the lower east side of New York. That actually was what gave him the inspiration to invent the CHUNKY chocolate bar. His customers and their consumers were mostly Jewish as was the lower east side area. Jewish people, he believed, loved chocolate with nuts and raisins. He was right! So began the CHUNKY saga.

Our first meeting was uneventful. Most significant was the frank appraisal we made of each other. Phil, at that time, was an inch over five feet. It seemed his circumference was the same dimension. He was, to be kind, rotund, chubby and close to 60 years old. His personality was arrogant and obstinate.

I, on the other hand, was 6 feet 2 inches tall and weighed 160 pounds. I was 29 years old and fervently anxious to be in a branded business with possibilities of national distribution.

There was a stark contrast between us in every way. We almost never agreed upon the solution to any problem, or the best way to promote the product or market it. This, of course, led to many confrontations. Once when we were standing outside the "shipping platform" on the sidewalk of Ridge Street, Phil started shoving me and I shoved back, and when the shouting rose to a high pitch, someone called the police. We wound up at the local police station near Delancey Street and were both admonished by the desk sergeant and discharged. It was truly comical, but we both learned a lesson, and never again did anything like that happen.

It was instantly apparent that physical dimensions were the least of our differences. We each came from a different culture, a different geography and from different generations. We thought differently and were diametrically different in our relationships with employees, suppliers, customers and each other.

I quickly took over the executive and administrative functions, which Phil ceded willingly.

On the second floor the mixing/heating kettles were located. There were two of them, four feet in diameter, water-jacketed with mixing blades.

Ten pound blocks of chocolate, as sent from the chocolate manufacturers, were wrapped in brown paper, and ten of them shipped in a burlap bag. (This was soon modernized to buying liquid chocolate shipped from the chocolate suppliers in tank trucks.)

First the wrapped blocks had to be removed from the bag. Then the paper wrap had to be torn off, and the chocolate blocks then broken by hitting them against the rim of the steel kettle. Hot water was fed into the jacket of the kettles and the resulting heat and mixing motion melted the chocolate into a viscous liquid. The odor in the room was like being submerged in a chocolate milkshake and the heat in this small room was intense. Here the nuts and raisins were mixed into the liquid chocolate,

The chocolate had to be carefully "tempered." This meant heating the chocolate first to about 110 degrees, and then carefully cooling it down to about 88 degrees so that the complex chocolate crystals would be properly formed. Otherwise it would not be in proper condition for molding into the Chunky pyramid shape.

Then the mixture was fed into a stainless steel pipe, which ran through the floor and emptied into a metal hopper below.

GRAVITY IS SO DEPENDABLE.

The stainless steel molds were pushed, one behind the other under the hopper, and the mixture dropped into the 12 CHUNKY shapes in the molds. The molds then went onto a moving conveyor belt, which ran through the cooling tunnel. The trip took about 20 minutes. At the end, the molds with the solidified chocolate bars were then removed by hand and the candy was knocked out by hitting the edge of the molds on a resilient block so that the candy could be fed into each of the four antique wrapping machines which wrapped them with aluminum foil printed with a red CHUNKY logo.

Including storage, inventory, shipping and office, the plant consisted of about 10,000 square feet. This was certainly a compact factory, to say the least.

At the time I took over the operation of Chunky, there was only one employee who was able to process the chocolate properly.

Several days after I began, on one of my visits to the chocolate mixing operation, Anthony, the mixer, confronted me. Placing his hand, possessively, on one of the kettles he told me he had to have a large raise. It was out of the question, but he was the only one who knew how to temper the chocolate. How could we continue operations without Anthony?

Well, the tough decision had to be made and Anthony was refused his demand and left the company. The next weeks were rather frantic as I was advising several potential "candy makers" how to temper chocolate, and handle the cashews and raisins which were the other ingredients in a CHUNKY candy bar. While it was a bit delicate, tempering chocolate properly is not exactly in the same class as rocket science, and soon a man was in place who could satisfactorily fill the job.

Shortly after the tempering crisis, the next one occurred. A person appropriately named Fat Al drove up in his 1948 Cadillac and announced that he was the union representative and he was going to represent the workers—all four of them. Fat Al's last name was never known, and he was a jolly fellow, well over 300 pounds on his six-foot frame. He liked nothing better than to have lunch while talking about unionizing the factory.

He didn't seem to have any other plants that he represented, nor did he have an affiliation with any union. After a number of lunches, and our agreement to pay his "expenses" he quietly went away.

Operations continued satisfactorily and sales grew rather quickly. I set our goal for growth at 3% per year. That was very small, especially when starting from zero, but I knew we could easily better that, and I wanted a goal that our staff could proudly come back and show me how much they beat it. A little reverse psychology.

The fast growth soon made the Delancey Street factory obsolete. A new plant was urgently needed. As usual, there was no money available but I was able to buy a building at Dean and Vanderbilt streets in Brooklyn. This was an old Ward Baking Co. bread plant (an interesting coincidence—see Chapter 19). Hooray! We finally had a receiving area, a shipping platform, and an adequate area for incoming trucks.

Of course it wasn't perfect, but it was a lot better than our previous "factory". The cooling segment of the material in the Chunky truncated pyramid molds required at least 20 minutes to get to the proper solid state. The new building was much too short to run a cooling tunnel the necessary length, so we built a cold room and a multi-level conveyor. This constantly was troublesome and bothered us for years.

The single greatest factor in producing a chocolate candy bar like Chunky is the cost of chocolate. Chunky never made its own chocolate. It had to purchase it from the manufacturers of chocolate. They, of course, purchased and ground the cocoa beans, added milk and sugar, in the case of milk chocolate added extra cocoa butter, and conged (ground) the mixture to produce chocolate of various grades.

Chunky had to negotiate contracts for chocolate with the chocolate manufacturers—mostly Hooton, Blumenthal, Walter Baker, and Ambrosia. They would then contract for the purchase of the equivalent quantity of cocoa beans. Grown near the Equator in Africa and South America, the beans varied greatly in quality, taste and cost. While marketing was always in the spotlight, purchasing the chocolate at a cost which enabled Chunky to sell candy at the competitive weight and price was the only way to assure a satisfactory bottom line. Although nuts and raisins were mixed in varying proportions, chocolate was always the basic commodity of Chunky.

Most companies employed experts to do this purchasing, which, of course, we could not afford. So I had to take on this responsibility. Typical of the cocoa bean market, there were tremendous increases and decreases at various times depending on the weather, world conditions, usage and supplies. For example, between the years of 1946 and 1947 beans rose from 12 cents to 34 cents per pound. In 1953 the price was 37 cents, and in 1954 exploded to an incredible 57 cents per pound. The usual contracts for chocolate I purchased were for $500,000 to $1,000,000. The wholesale selling price of a box of candy bars to the trade could never be based on what we had to pay for chocolate, the essential commodity. It was quite the opposite. Our wholesale selling price was rigidly established by the market. What all the manufacturers were charging the trade for a box of five-cent bars (later 10 cents) established the price we could afford to pay for chocolate. Unfortunately, this had to be decided in advance, sometimes as far as a year in advance. Even an expert economist knows the danger of forecasting anything a year in advance. Nevertheless, in over 20 years, we never paid more than that which enabled us to profit at our usual expected rate. Chalk that up to one part luck and one part diligence.

Our new factory was a five-story building and had excellent space for the office on the fifth floor. The office staff grew to 15 and the factory employed over 100. These factory workers were eventually unionized by the C.I.O.

CHAPTER 9

GETTING STARTED

**Delancey Street
Manhattan, NY
February, 1951**

Okay—I had my company. It was something I longed for. I loved the word entrepreneur, and now I was one. Well, it was really only one-half of a company. How could I acquire the other half and be rid of the inhibiting presence of Phil Silvershein with all of the problems that entailed?

Back to that very nice mother-in-law, this time for $40,000*. That was not an insignificant sum of money in 1951, and to me it loomed like a mountain over my every thought. How fast could I pay back the $65,000? What would this now just-out-of-bankruptcy company have to sell to make enough profits to liquidate the loans? How could I even consider such a move? After all, I was just a wet-behind-the-ears entrepreneur in a business long run by major brands. How could I compete with the big guys? What reason would a buyer

---

*$329,800 in 2009 dollars—AIER

of candy bars have for ordering a chocolate bar with nuts and raisins in a funny shape, instead of a Hershey chocolate bar or a Nestle Crunch?

On the first day I went out to sell, and I was the only salesman as well as the only active executive in all departments, the buyer of the Union News Co. in New York gave me some advice. "That's a very interesting shape," he said, "but you should flatten it out and make it look as large as a Hershey bar."

His advice led to a serious dilemma. He wanted me to copycat the original Hershey Bar.

One of the ways I sold was to simply ask what they thought about my product. Some had unusual arguments against Chunky. But others talked themselves into liking the shape. Trying to sell a new product amidst major brands was not easy. There were always those potential buyers who could not see the value of a believable point of difference. They were indeed a hindrance to moving forward. But slowly, with a small order here, and another there, I began to see that there indeed was a tiny space for CHUNKY. I could see a bit of light there and then, a number of small openings. Each one is an opportunity.

How to take advantage and move forward? There were critical times. There was no money and no history of success I could use as a reference. To make it more difficult there was really no clear path to follow. So I had to explore each resistant opportunity and try to make a sale. Some felt the CHUNKY was not too small but it was too thick. Others felt it was not thick enough but too small. In talking to buyers, some felt it was either too big, or had an undesirable shape, or just was not thick enough. Heck, it's only a Chunky, I would say in response. Then I would offer this analogy: It tastes better than a paper-thin chocolate bar, Mr. Buyer. Thick just the way you know that a thick steak tastes better than a thin one.

In discussing the merits and demerits of Chunky, I had come full circle. I began to realize I was not selling just candy. I was selling taste!

However, instinctively, I realized that the truncated pyramid shape of a Chunky was unique and offered an unusual opportunity to have a distinctly different selling point. It was a perfect example of what the famed ad guru—Rosser Reeves of the Ted Bates advertising agency would later call "a Unique Selling Proposition," better known in that trade as USP. Or what I would always call a believable point of difference.

So for better or worse, I stayed with the shape. It was unquestionably the single most important decision I ever made for the future success of Chunky. Many buyers had resistance at first, but eventually came to see that Chunky had a place on the candy shelves of the retail stores and theaters. Several other flat Hershey-like chocolate bars came on the market, but eventually went out of business.

The next step was to figure to get the consumers to buy the product off the shelves. Even though they were not very aggressive, there was a tremendous amount of competition out there.

The answer was fairly obvious. We had to tell the end-user about our tasty Chunky product. We had to advertise.

But getting the money for advertising was not so simple. Chunky was always a bootstrap operation. A dollar spent for advertising meant a dollar less for a new desperately needed wrapping machine. Cash flow problems were always at hand. It required critical decisions every day.

The first "national" advertising budget for Chunky was $13,000 for a 13week exposure on the Freddie Robbins Show. Freddie was a disc jockey and had a combination talk and music show televised over one local New York station. Not much exposure for a wannabe national product, but it was a beginning.

CHAPTER 10

ESPRIT DE CORPS

> **655 Dean St.**
> **Brooklyn, NY**
> **1952**

When you put together a turnaround rescue operation of a
so-so branded product with young, inexperienced people
fighting against old, established and rich companies, you
have to have lots of energy, conviction, spirit and dedication to specific and clearly defined goals.

Now these characteristics are not uncommon in most businesses,
but in a new situation such as CHUNKY, everyone has to be at the
very top level. The few people who left or were fired were simply
unable to summon the needed level of these characteristics. They
were not "hungry" enough, or did not consider the challenge to fur-
nish enough opportunity and reward.

The passionate development and protection of a brand was holy.
That said it all. A brand was gold—a solid base. The brand's strength
sheltered everything. A bad batch, a weak ad, a poor sales effort, as

harmful as all these things might be, could be turned to good. But not without limit.

A brand name is a composite of many things. First you have the product. But to enhance it you need the right packaging. This must be logically followed by consistent methods of distribution, a continuity of quality, and obtaining a niche at its own level which may be, and really should be, different. It could be higher or lower than competing brands, or even brands in other categories or industries.

Finally there is the reputation of the company, its executives, and its place in the industry. Is it a "me too," or does it offer something different? Does it have a U.S.P., a Unique Selling Proposition? Could you remove this product from an advertisement and put a competitive product in its place without a noticeable difference?

I had engraved a credo for the company on small desk plaques "PROFITS FOLLOW THE PURSUIT OF EXCELLENCE January 1, 1966." I truly gloried in the right—nay, the obligation—to make a decision. In fact I reserved the right to make almost all decisions for CHUNKY. But my decisions were never made in a complete vacuum. I would use suggestions by the minimal staff we had. Many offered constructive suggestions. Others had novice ideas that required development. Whatever the case, I had to make the ultimate decision. To do that, I would also attempt to offer constructive alternatives to a staffer's suggestions and turn them into gold. It was my personal treasure, and even if a decision was wrong I still felt comfort in the ability to take charge and to be responsible and maintain that special sense of integrity.

The study of management has evolved over decades and most schools now have similar courses, case studies and lectures.

The elements of good management usually leave out, or skip by, what I consider to be the first requisite—COMMON SENSE. It is rarely mentioned. It is not taught in classes. It really cannot be taught at all. It is genetic.

The next characteristic necessary for a good manager is Dedication. It can be learned, but I have always suspected it is partly genetic too. There are many "Time-Putters" who consider that to be "dedicated" is merely putting in time. Time alone is not nearly sufficient. There can be no easing up. There can be no finessing the input we received and certainly no over-delegating or using favorite pathways or friendly considerations. Sometimes suggestions that appeared beneficial at first glance were proven to be extremely fuzzy, or without focus.

True DEDICATION requires a full commitment of mind, heart and soul. Then follows the traditional list from your favorite Management School, with which I surely would agree, and, by the way, never forget CREATIVITY. That should be high on anyone's list.

At one point during the Chunky years, I sent a questionnaire to the entire staff offering them an opportunity to rate me, the CEO, in a dozen or more categories. The result was not too surprising. The category which I received the highest rating was "ability to select good subordinates."

To successfully lead my team meant to inspire them. It was not my style to be a cheerleader. I was not one for all hype and no substance. That is why I felt that the best way was to set an example. Often someone would explain that they were doing "the best that they could." That was never satisfactory.

It is no use saying,
"We are doing our best"
You have got to succeed in doing
what is necessary.

—Winston S. Churchill
British Prime Minister

It truly never crossed my mind that I would not succeed. Failure was an option not contemplated, even in such a perilous effort as building a national brand, without money, no less, and in a mature, competitive industry. Looking back, I suppose it was the confidence of youth, the confidence of self and the strong sense that there was an opportunity. These characteristics permeated through out the organization and resulted in a quiet inspiration.

CHAPTER 11

PARK, LEXINGTON AND THIRD, BUT NOT MADISON AVENUE

> **Manhattan, NY**
> **1946-1985**

Working with advertising agencies was constant throughout my career.

Beginning when I was in the advertising department of Tootsie Rolls and ultimately Advertising Manager, my first experience was with the Duane Jones Advertising Agency. This was a new boutique agency, very small but a highly creative operation. An experienced ad man was the account executive, and his assistant was a typical young mid-westerner who came east to New York and found his way into advertising. They were both solid and productive.

This was the Golden Age of the influence of ad agencies in the burgeoning growth of post World War II American industry. While some agencies resided on the famed Mecca of Madison Avenue, many did not. Duane Jones was on Lexington Avenue. It was successful until internal dissention of account control led to its breakup.

Advertising expenditures for confectionery products jumped 46% in 1975 to a record $49 million.* The top five confectionery advertisers spent $32 million during 1975, or 65% of total industry advertising. M & M/Mars accounted for 20% of all outlays, representing a decline from 30% in 1970.

The industry as a whole rapidly increased its use of television advertising. In those days it accounted for almost 96% of all major media ads.

At Chunky, its first agency was Peck Advertising also on Lexington Avenue. Starting with its first "national" ad budget of $13,000, it slowly grew to at least satisfactory coverage of Chunky's major market.

The next agency was Grey Advertising. This agency, located on Park Avenue, was, at that time, a mid-sized operation which took Chunky advertising to all of its major markets in the U.S. The budget eventually grew to $1,000.000.**

Grey also began using "celebrities" for the ads. They introduced Arnold Stang, who enthusiastically made "What a chunk of chocolate" into a happy slogan. Then came Abbott & Costello who gave the slogan and the brand great status and appreciation.

Next, we edged our way into the big time with J. Walter Thompson, on Lexington Ave., then the second largest ad agency in the U.S. and perhaps the world. They did a consistently solid job. I realized that we were just a minor player with aspirations to compete with the big boys. But we were constantly growing and becoming a significant part of the candy industry.

---

*$195,279,000 in 2009 dollars—AIER
**$7,243,000 in 2009 dollars—AIER

Later, at Schrafft, we found Warren Pfaff, a terrific small agency on Park Avenue, which made the mundane "Have we got a candy for you!" into a very successful campaign.

There were never any "two martini" lunches or even one martini. In fact there were never lunches or entertainment of any kind. It was all business in our office or theirs.

There was always the question of whether we should spend money on market research. Market research was a proven way to help insure successful advertising or justify the use for specific appeals in advertising. However, we always used our limited funds for advertising.

The ad agencies were:

> Creative—sometimes
>
> Effective—mostly
>
> Difficult—always.

We worked with many bright, creative and dedicated account executives. They were, with few exceptions, all willing and excited purveyors of the products they promoted. We, the advertisers, as clients, had to provide input and ultimately make the final creative decision. The advertising decisions were almost always made by Al Erlich, Ken Jaffe, my brother, and me. Marathon meetings, often lasting long into the night, characterized these sessions. But it was fun and great to enjoy seeing the successful results amplify the bottom line.

Ken Jaffe, my younger brother, felt, as I did, that working for the Jaffe uncles in Washington was limited. He came to New York after his stint in the army and began working at Chunky. He did a fine job in purchasing and marketing and was a great asset for Chunky. However I felt that he was too bright, too competent, and too ambitious to continue to work for me. Hopefully, I would be around for a long time before he could become head of the company. He and I agreed that he should have his own company and he founded and headed a successful advertising agency for over 40 years.

Comedian Arnold Stang with Jaffe

Kenneth Jaffe

Jeff Jaffe

CHAPTER 12

THIS SHAPE SELLS CANDY

**June 1950
NCWA Convention
Chicago, IL**

There were two national conventions that most candy manufacturers attended every year. These were the NCWA, known as the National Confectionery Wholesalers Association and the NATD, known as the National Association of Tobacco Distributors.

The NCWA in 1950 was the very first opportunity for Chunky to reach a large number of potential customers.

Alvin Erlich had appeared a few months before. He walked in the door at Delancey Street looking for a job. No experience, but I liked the "cut of his jib." He was hired at $50 a week as an administrative assistant. This proved to be one of the best decisions I ever made. While Al's title of VP of Marketing indicated his responsibility for Sales and Advertising, he and I were in frequent communication about other matters. We regularly had lunch two or three times a week and rarely discussed anything but business. We learned to work together and he was a vital factor in the success of the companies. He ultimately became Executive Vice President of Chunky and later President of the Ward Foods Candy & Biscuit Group.

Aleck Abrahamson was for many years a Sales Vice President of the Tootsie Roll Company. His modus operandi was traveling eleven months of the year. He had become disenchanted with the presidency of Bill Rubin and left Tootsie Rolls. I was delighted to have him join us at Chunky where he immeasurably improved and maintained relations with our customers. He was an important factor in our growth and, with Erlich, built a strong confectionery broker-age organization. This was extremely vital to the success of the company. He never flew but only traveled by train. He was beloved by the customers and invariably was always invited to their homes for dinner. He wrote hundreds of post cards to customers. After his passing we set up and sponsored the annual "Golden Post Card Award" in his memory to honor the "Candy Wholesaler of the Year."

As always, money was a problem when I decided to exhibit at the NCWA. We had to rent a booth, design and build a display and pay for four days in a hotel in Chicago. For the display we purchased a plastic sculpture. It was a Venus—like torso of a woman with an attractive nude body. No head, no legs or arms, and no details of her breast or pubic areas. That was to be placed in the left side of our display with a sign saying:

"THIS SHAPE CAN SELL ANYTHING"

On the right side of the display was one giant wrapped Chunky with a sign saying:

"BUT THIS SHAPE SELLS CANDY"

The display was a hit and got us many favorable comments and, more importantly, resulted in a good amount of orders.

However, the Executive Director of the Association told us that our display of Venus was indecent. He said we had to remove it. Naturally we strongly objected and finally compromised that we could keep it if we covered her pubic area. Actually this got us a great deal of extra attention and humorous comments.

So much for the prudish morality in the 1950s.

Historically, except for the largest manufacturers, candy bar lines were sold by Manufacturer Representatives, a fancy term for candy brokers. In every case the brokers represented several companies. Even though each candy bar line competed with each other brand, each customer always bought many brands of candies, and this allowed multiple representation by the brokers. It was efficient and actually helped the customers as they could buy from only one salesman instead of three or four who would represent three or four candy companies.

Shortly after Chunky began selling on a national basis, we appointed brokers to cover the entire nation. We began with about 20 in all. All of the brokers carried several other brands in addition to Chunky, and three of them also sold Tootsie Rolls.

There was Harry Green in Washington-Baltimore; Sid Goldberg in metropolitan New York, and Julius Dehm. Julius was arguably the largest candy broker in the country. He covered Chicago, Detroit and contiguous territories.

Shortly after their appointments were made public, each received an ultimatum from the Tootsie Roll Company. The ultimatum was that they had to give up Chunky or they would no longer represent the Tootsie Roll line. This was just another example of Bill Rubin's small-minded jealousy. I certainly didn't expect any help from Tootsie

Rolls, but it was not at all unusual for candy companies to share brokers.

Well, how far did this jealous show of strength get them?

Sid Goldberg sorrowfully decided to resign the Chunky line. When we discussed it, I told Sid that I understood his predicament. He left Chunky but we were still friends. He was replaced by DeWitt Cottrell whose company sold a greater volume of Chunkys than Tootsie Rolls ever did. It did take him about a year to beat the volume.

Harry Green took a different course. He resigned the Tootsie Roll line and went on to substantially greater sales with Chunky.

Julius Dehm, the patriarch of candy brokers, refused to give up either, and Bill Rubin was powerless, and in my opinion, became the laughingstock of the industry. I always had a special love for these brokers.

As Chunky became a basic consumer product, we had to be aware of all the new trends that could affect our business. We began to realize that the trend towards dieting was growing and had become popular at all age levels. Since candy was always known to be relatively high in calories, we had to develop a way of meeting this upcoming consumer demand.

We began working with a food laboratory to develop a "low calorie" candy bar. It was unveiled and presented to the public at a trade show in New York City.

Shortly after its introduction, a representative of the FTC came to the Chunky office and ordered the "Sweet 'n Low" candy bar to be withdrawn from the market. They claimed that its stated 35% reduction in calories was not enough to market it on the "lower in calories" basis. We did not agree. We said that the market should determine the efficacy of the product. But the FTC would not relent and we had to discontinue the product. I always felt that the powerful sugar companies were responsible for that governmental edict.

One of the best promotions I instituted was a panel of Candy Tasters. This consisted of hundreds of young children around the country who each received a different Chunky product once a month. They then sent in a written report to the company. The "word of mouth" advertising was terrific.

HOW SWEET IT IS

JEFF JAFFE
CHUNKY CHOCOLATE CORPORATION

O**NCE UPON A TIME...**

DEEP IN THE FOREST OF HEWLETT BAY PARK THERE LIVED A FAMILY OF JAFFS...

(a Jaff dear reader, is someone who is not yet out of the woods)

JEFF	NATALIE	BONNIE	HOLLY	WAFFLES & SYRUP

There was Papa Jaff	and Mama Jaff	and two Little Jaffs		There was live stock too

Now bright and early every morning Papa Jaff rides from the forest and goes to that place from which he brings home the ~~bacon~~ *Chunkys*. (If it seems like he keeps bankers' hours, it's only because the banks own most of the business anyhow ...

He sometimes goes to his office in Manhattan, or to his old established factory in Brooklyn.

Or even to another one in Chicago. In fact most of the time he doesn't know where-in-hell he's going.

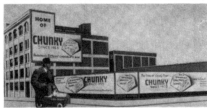

Chunky plant (since 1953)

Schutter plant

He makes many kinds of ... bacon

This is extremely difficult & tedious	And often unpleasant	In fact it is nothing but ...		
		Work!	Work!	Work!

Over 1,000 business biographics were submitted at the Greenbrier convention and this was the *only one* selected to be in the 50th Anniversary book published by YPO.

THIS SHAPE SELLS CANDY

YOUNG PRESIDENTS' ORGANIZATION

Many nice people often help him get rid of all this bacon (His inventory is usually too high)

IT'S TOO SMALL!

TOO MANY RAISINS!

Most people clamor for Chunkys

IT COSTS TOO MUCH!

NOT ENOUGH RAISINS!

He sometimes works for Charitable Organizations

He carries such a great load

He is also an avid sportsman

Fishing

Boating

Skiing

Mountain climbing

Golfing

Corn husking

When he finally returns home weary from a hard day's work The Jaffs relax at the old homestead.

L-R: Mort Singer, Al Erlich, Jaffe, Aleck Abrahamson

Jaffe with Sweet'n Low Model

RETAILERS GUIDE

TOBACCO & CONFECTIONERY DEALER

Editorial and Business Offices—50 Court Street, Brooklyn 1, N. Y.

Telephone: MAin 4-3354

Published on the 15th of every month at North Hackensack, New Jersey. Subscription Price — $3.00 a year.

Everett Einarsen	Editor & Publisher
Hamilton Pitt	New England Editor
Paul Lockwood	West Coast Editor
James McClanaghan	Mid West Editor
M. L. Schwartz	Canadian Editor

JANUARY, 1954   VOL. XXII NO. 1

Chunky Chocolates Launches New, Low-Calorie Chocolate

A DECISIVE WAY TO EXPAND CANDY SALES

To meet the increased public demand for lower-calorie foods, the Devan Candy Division of Chunky Chocolate Corp., announced a new product, "Sweet 'n Low", a chocolate bar containing less calories. "Sweet 'n Low" will be the first chocolate bar developed for the weight conscious market.

Speaking at a press luncheon, Jeff Jaffe, president of the Chunky Chocolate, said, " 'Sweet 'n Low' will appeal to the many calorie-conscious people who have scratched candy from their diets because of weight control. We at Chunky are certain 'Sweet 'n Low' will prove a decisive means of expanding candy consumption in the United States.

"Our industry has been one of the chief victims of the present emphasis on low-calorie, non-fattening foods. Candy especially chocolate candy, is a nutritious, energy-giving food. It contains a lot of calories. In 'Sweet 'n Low', we have found a way to reduce the calorie content by substituting non-caloric substances for the usual high-calorie sweetening agents. Each bar gives the consumer the taste satisfaction of having eaten a regular candy bar and at the same time is less fattening!"

Mr. Jaffe described the long, arduous experimentation involved before a suitable, acceptable formula for "Sweet 'n Low" finally emerged. For over a year, chemists of an independent food research organization mixed batch after batch of chocolate combined with varying degrees of substitute sweeteners. The laboratory workers and office staff at Chunky soon became accustomed to their roles as taste testers for the many combinations.

"Some were downright terrible," Jaffe recalled. "Too bitter, too sweet, too thick, too thin, too crunchy, and sometimes — too strange! But we finally hit on the right mixture about two months ago. It meets all our specifications for low calorie content and real taste appeal. We selected the name 'Sweet 'n Low' for the obvious reasons of good eating and low-calorie content. We are confident it will catch on and lure thousands of new consumers back to the candy-eating habit while encouraging wider consumption among the general public."

Reviewing statistics compiled by leading insurance companies, Mr. Jaffe concluded, "Over 35 million Americans are an average of 16 pounds overweight — a total of 560 million pounds of unnecessary weight in the country today.

"We are not going to sit back and watch an increasingly weight-conscious consuming public remove candy from their everyday enjoyment. 'Sweet n' Low' is our answer."

CHAPTER 13

WORLD'S LARGEST SELLING CANDY BAR

Brooklyn, N.Y.
York, England
1951-1967

One day I received a call from an Englishman, Walter Crossley, who advised that he and Robert MacCauley were visiting the United States on a mission to find a company to import Kit Kat, their world's best-selling candy bar. Crossley, a very proper Englishman, was Sales Vice President of Rowntree & Co. of York, England, and had heard of Chunky through Candy Industry magazine, a trade paper for the confectionery industry. MacCauley was plant manager at York.

After several meetings a temporary agreement was reached and the CHUNKY organization would import KIT KAT into the United States.

This was in 1951. CHUNKY was a very young, fledgling operation and was excited about being associated with a giant international company like ROWNTREE, one of the largest confectioners in the world.

Arrangements for the import and distribution of Kit Kat went smoothly and the agreement was made permanent. Their beautiful motto was "Have a Break, Have A Kit Kat," and was known throughout the world.

Over the years I made many trips to visit Rowntree, located in York, about 2½ hours north of London by the very active railroad. In 1954, there was very little city to city flying in England and there was always the Station Hotel at the railroad station. It was the largest and best hotel in each city.

York was truly an ancient city, many centuries old. It was captured by the Romans in 71 AD, and they built a solid brick wall completely around the city, a lot of which is still standing. During the olden days, workers of a similar trade were banded together in various guilds. The Merchant Adventurers Hall, one of the oldest guild halls, was built in 1357. We worked together and decided many of the business considerations for marketing Kit Kat. The York factory was huge and I confess to being in awe of the plant's enormity. Frankly I was amazed with every aspect of Rowntree during my first visit to that unique facility. There were 10,000 employees in York and a thousand more in a 250,000 square foot building in Newcastle. The York factory occupied a number of buildings consisting of 2 million square feet in a park-like setting of 250 acres not including the Rowntree Village of New Eastwick.

The machinery and equipment was then "state of the art" and the management and personnel walked and talked with high morale in spite of the very paternalistic system under which they worked.

Rowntree was an interesting company. Its Board of Directors were individually based in York and were completely active in the operations of the company. Ownership of the company shares was substantially held by the Rowntree Trusts to which the shares had been dedicated by the Rowntree family. These trustees were invisible.

During my first visit to York in 1954, I was invited to lunch in the Directors' Dining Room. There I was sitting with ten Directors, very formal, very serious and very intimidating.

But they were warm and friendly and stood up to make several speeches assuring me of Rowntree's need for Chunky to provide Kit Kat's successful entrée into the U.S. market. I then stood to make a short speech of agreement and pleasure at being associated with such an outstanding company. We had come to enjoy each other's company. There was never a WRITTEN CONTRACT with them. It was simply done with a handshake.

The firm of Rowntree dates from Henry Isaac Rowntree's purchase of a cocoa, chocolate and chicory business from his former employer in July 1862 at that time employing a dozen men. Sales were about £3000.*

In 1869, Joseph joined the firm and established a business-like and solid foundation. The Rowntrees were Quakers and followed the principle that the products were to be of the highest quality and refused to make false claims about their goods,

The company was commited to operate with only the highest ethics. They were very paternalistic which provided justification for the exercise of an authority, which was part cultural, part force of economic circumstances between employer and employed, and part matter of law.

Their "office block" consisted of an imposing separate building designed in a traditional style. The first floor was one very large room filled with the desks of at least 60 secretaries and assistants. There were no separate offices or partitions. The second floor housed

*Rowntree—The Marketing Revolution by Robert Fitzgerald.

the private offices of the senior executives on a balcony surrounding and overlooking the first floor. A "tea lady" made the rounds mid-morning and mid-afternoon with their delicious milk-laced tea which tasted different and better than in America. A large conference room was on the balcony. This was where I spent virtually all my time in continuous meetings with various executives. It was there that I learned the differences in our language. For example, to "table" an item in American means to put it on hold. In English, it means to discuss it now.

The very use of this word occasioned a lively fifteen-minute skirmish as we all made a brave attempt to reach rational communication.

*Thomas Jefferson embraced the development
of an indigenous American language,
arguing that everyday usage is the workshop in which
new words are elaborated rather than English dictionaries
compiled by the likes of Samuel Johnson.
John Adams declared "All English dictionaries were
vestiges of the same British tyranny that the American
Revolution destroyed forever."**

Later, during their visit to America, Lloyd Owen, Rowntree Chairman and CEO, and his wife Gladys, had dinner with us at our home in Hewlett Bay Park, on Long Island. Interestingly, my wife Natalie served corn on the cob to the amazement of the Owens who, as English, always believed that it was only fit for animals. With some trepidation, they managed to eat the corn in the American style.

*Founding Brothers—Joseph J. Ellis

On the table, Natalie had placed several small dishes of candy, as was her custom when we had guests for dinner. In this instance the candy was Wallace Wafer Thin Mints. The Owens had never seen anything like these mints before and after eating some at the end of dinner, extended comments of great praise.

Nothing was ever said to me at any time after about the candy by Lloyd. Several months later I received a call from my friend Herb Bebar, president of Wallace, who asked me about Lloyd Owen and Rowntree. He told me he had been contacted by Rowntree who were interested in working out a deal to produce the Thin Mints in England. They were never able to work out an agreeable contract with Wallace, so they developed the product themselves. It became a major staple for them as one of their best selling products. Never did Lloyd, or anyone else at Rowntree, acknowledge that I introduced them to Thin Mints.

Later, when I was President, I bought the Wallace business for Schraffts.

Chunky was successful in achieving nationwide distribution of Kit Kat in a short time. In addition to our sales and marketing efforts, it was the quality of the product and its very different chocolate covered sugar wafer center which resulted in immediate acceptance by the trade and consumers. Its sales growth was impressive.

The hard work and many assets which Chunky devoted to achieving this success was costly and did not cover the start-up expenses. However, it augured well for the future profits which Chunky anticipated.

All of us in the UK and in the U.S.A. believed strongly that if you reach your goals, you will collect your reward! This was the certainty that purveyed my meetings with Lloyd Owen, Chairman, Raymond Clifford, Marketing Director, and Walter Crossley, the Sales

Director of Rowntree. This certainty, amidst all the competition and problems that one could have, was surely embedded in all our efforts. Surely, positively! Well, maybe. We'll see.

Raymond Clifford—Marketing Director of Rowntree
and Walter Crossley, Sales Director with Jaffe—Brooklyn, N.Y.

L-R: Lloyd and Gladys Owen—Natalie and Jeff—
Plaza Hotel, New York, N.Y.

Rowntree Executive Directors with Jaffe

Raymond Clifford-Marketing
Walter Crossley-Sales
Mons Bentsson-Finance
Lloyd Owen-Chairman
William Porteous-Advertising
Ralph Kaner-Marketing

CHAPTER 14

DEUCE OR PAR

Inwood Country Club
Inwood, Long Island
April, 1954

Ellsworth Vines was the tennis champion in 1934 and '35 at Forest Hills, N.Y., and Wimbledon, England. In those days amateurism reigned, and tennis victors received a trophy and a headline but no money. In the 30's there were no million dollar tennis prizes, in fact no monetary prizes at all.

So to make a living, Ellsworth turned to golf and briefly played on the PGA tour, despite knowing that tennis was his all-consuming priority. He became a competent professional golfer, but because of his late start, he never achieved greatness. Wisely, he became a golf club professional at Inwood, Long Island in the summer and at Tamarisk in Palm Springs, California in the winter.

Natalie and I joined Inwood in 1954 and we immediately began taking lessons from Ellsworth. He had developed into an excellent teacher with an uncanny ability to peer through the thicket of bad swings and produce solutions for each yearning student. I began with a handicap of 31 and Natalie a 36.

She ultimately won runner-up in class A, and I won class B. Ellie and I played together often, and he incessantly challenged me with comments like, "I know you'll out-drive me, but my ball will be in the fairway." Golf became our favorite activity and we spent many happy years at Inwood.

LONG ISLAND PRESS, TUESDAY SEPTEMBER 11, 1962

Vines, Aided by Jaffe, Makes 'Em Forget Net

By JOHN M. BRENNAN

There used to be a time when Ellsworth Vines was the toast of the tennis world. He was champion at Wimbledon and Forest Hills. Yesterday while the racquet wielding fans had their eyes focused on the turf courts at Forest hills as the national title was being decided, Vines was cast in a far different role.

Vines, now a golf pro at Inwood Country Club, appeared oblivious as what was happening at Forest Hills. In fact, he was out stroking the golf ball in the LIPGA's pro-amateur 1962 Championship being staged over the hand- some course at North Hempstead Country Club, Port Washington.

Vines when he was playing tennis, was mostly on his own –and winning. Yesterday, in the tandem event, he needed assistance, but this was adequately furnished by Jeff Jaffe, who used eight strokes handicap advantage to give the Inwood team the net prize with a nine-under 62.

Jaffe proved a great helpmate to the former tennis whiz. In fact, Jeff produced an eagle, with the aid of a stroke, at the 11th. The amateur also came to Vines' assistance at the fourth, sixth, seventh, ninth, 14th and 15th. Ellsworth had a 74 on his own ball. The team had 31 on each nine.

Masters Tournament—Augusta, Georgia, Sports Illustrated—1994

Meet You At 7

A day spent by the 7th hole offers golf both sweet and sour and a taste of Augusta etiquette
by John Garrity

"WHERE'S JAFFE?" asked a man standing under the loblolly pines behind the 7th green at Augusta National.

"*You* could be Jaffe," his companion replied.

It was Saturday, shortly before noon, and the two men were eyeing an empty canvas-and-aluminum chair two rows behind the ropes and dead behind the pin. The owner's name, Jaffe, was on the backrest in black ink.

It is Masters tradition that spectators can claim greenside spots by planting chairs in the designated areas. But there is no requirement that they actually sit in them. Jaffe's seat, and the one next to it, had been unoccupied since 9 a.m.

So "You could be Jaffe" became a running gag for a few spectators among the

hundreds gathered around the 7th green. A couple of British punters made a "When will Jaffe get here?" wager. Inquiring minds asked, *"Who* is Jaffe?"

Then Jaffe arrived. A fit-looking older man in a white sweater, glasses and a Masters hat, Jeff Jaffe stood for a while with his wife, Natalie, behind their seats, unaware that he had become a minor celebrity. A man in a terry-cloth hat hailed him and said, "If I'd known they were *your* seats, I'd have sat in them."

Jaffe, of Greenwich, Conn., and Stuart, Fla., turned out to be a man of sweet disposition—literally. "I used to make candy bars," he said. Specifically, he once owned the Chunky Corporation, proud makers of Chunky and Oh Henry! bars, Bit-O-Honey, Raisinets and Goobers. "Nestle owns those names now," Jaffe said. "I'm retired."

Once the Jaffes were seated, their neighbors could concentrate on golf.

_____. Before Jaffe and his wife left for the 15th hole, he was asked to describe the 7th-hole spectators in confectioner's terms. Were they Goobers or Chunkies or Bits-O-Honey? "People here are sweet, so I'd have to say Honeys," Jaffe said. "Most places, you leave your chair and somebody will steal it." ∎

95

CHAPTER 15

HONEY OF A DEAL

Office of Frank Prince
Fifth Avenue, New York
December, 1957

It came to my attention that the Schutter—Johnson Candy Co. in Chicago, was for sale. It was owned by Universal Match Co. of St. Louis. Schutter was an old and well-known firm in the industry. The company manufactured and sold two major brands of candy which had been marketed for over 40 years under the nationally known names of Bit O' Honey and Old Nick. Before World War II, Schutter Candy Co. had been one of the larger firms in the industry, but in the postwar years, sales had declined about 75% under a series of absentee managements. By 1957 Schutter Candy Co. was reported to be operating in the red, with its loss for the year expected to be in excess of $300,000.*

The manufacturing facility was located at the junction of Cicero and Augusta on the north side of Chicago. This was a very dense

---

* $2,289,000 in 2009 dollars—AIER

commercial area and, interestingly, very near the Williamson Candy Co. makers of Oh Henry and E.J. Brach, a very large major producer of many varieties of candies under the Brach label. Also nearby was the Leaf Candy Co., which also produced a large variety of candies.

Universal had acquired Schutter partly on the theory that its match salesmen could sell candy as well as matches. The customers were similar and the sales overhead would be reduced significantly. However, it just did not work out that way.

Progress of the Negotiations*

Chunky approached Universal about a possible purchase, saying "We have no money, but if you are interested, so are we." A short time later Universal asked Chunky to submit a plan of what it might do with the Schutter Candy Co.

The negotiations between Chunky and Frank Prince, largest stockholder of Universal Match Co., had four principal issues to resolve: (1) the payment schedule, (2) the amount of the down payment, (3) skepticism on the part of Universal Match that Chunky management could turn a "loser" into a profitable company, and (4) uncertainty on the part of Chunky's management as to whether it could, in fact, turn the business around in as short time as it hoped it could.

I jumped at the opportunity to acquire Schutter. The Bit-O-Honey brand was strong and provided a non-chocolate diversification for Chunky. The product was special and the package was unique. The wax paper divider was inter-laced between each of the six pieces of Bit-O-Honey.

---

*From Harvard Business School—Midway Foods cases about the Chunky companies.

After receiving the financial statements, Chunky's top management held a Saturday-Sunday (January 11-12) meeting at my home. Management reviewed the information and then drew up a statement of basic objectives and bargaining strategy, a projected profit and loss statement, and a projected cash flow statement.

Frank Prince and I had immediate consanguinity and he was a helpful negotiator.

As was always the case, Chunky did not have any free cash and our net worth was not significant. Nevertheless we worked out a deal whereby I could buy the company on a deferred, but fair basis.

We visited the plant, still maintaining our due diligence process and found it to be an excellent facility that produced the finished product cleanly and efficiently. It was overstaffed for the volume of candy it was selling and therefore was losing a lot of money. Administrative costs were high, typified in one small example by the records of percentage of sales by each candy broker carried to the fourth decimal place. Those numbers to the fourth decimal would have been funny if it were not so costly. I had to ask myself many times "What were they thinking?"

Major Problems

The Payment Schedule: Chunky insisted on a payment schedule which would permit purchase of Schutter Candy Co. out of the latter's anticipated future earnings. Chunky made it clear that its own tight financial position made any other form of payment impossible. As a result, several payment schedules were discussed, with expressed interest in a shorter repayment period, with the payments tapering off toward the end.

Working Capital Guarantee: Since Schutter Candy Co. was losing about $25,000 per month Universal Match had loaned $300,000* to Schutter Candy Co. for additional working capital. Universal Match insisted that any sales agreement contain Chunky's guarantee that Schutter Candy Co. working capital would go no lower than $244,000.** In the event that Chunky was unable to fulfill its obligations, it would be required to reimburse Schutter Candy Co. to bring working capital up to the $244,000 figure. Although Chunky originally declined to be bound by such a guarantee, in January it provisionally agreed to do so in return for a 50% reduction in the down payment, from $100,000 to $50,000.***

The Down Payment: Chunky attempted to find $50,000 needed for the down payment. The money was not available from company funds and could not be secured from either Chunky's or Schutter's banking connections or from any of Chunky's major suppliers. Subsequently, however, a Chunky customer agreed to provide the required cash and to accept repayment through a purchase discount.

Purchase Price: The purchase price had not been a major issue from Universal Match's point of view as long as it was in excess of book value. Two points were evident. First, Universal Match would receive at most only a $50,000 cash payment and the remainder from future earnings. Second, Universal Match's security in the deal rested upon Chunky's ability to turn a loser into a profitable company in order to generate these future earnings. Universal Match's major concern, therefore, was not the exact amount of the sale price but the likelihood that Chunky would actually make money on Schutter rather

---

In 2009 dollars—AIER

*$2,289,000

**$1.861,700

***$ 381,500

than "dumping it back into Universal Match's lap." The purchase price was not a major issue for Chunky since the amount would, in any event, have to come from future earnings.

Chunky's Corporate Objectives

The possible acquisition of Schutter would be consistent with some of Chunky's corporate objectives and inconsistent with some others.

The acquisition of two new brands would be consistent with Chunky's phase-one objective of growth. It would add over $2 million* to annual sales in staple brand name items. Future growth would depend on Chunky's marketing skills.

Also it would fit in with the objective of diversification in the candy industry, and was particularly suitable since Bit O' Honey would "act as a balance wheel."

However these two brands would require substantial advertising expenditures for two reasons (1) to halt their sales decline and (2) to become more profitable by regaining lost volume. While both brands were nationally known, distribution was spotty, with approximately 70% of Old Nick sales concentrated in the six-state New England area. Reintroducing this brand on a national basis would be, (in management's opinion) only slightly less difficult than introducing a new brand. For either to become a truly national brand would require some diversification of funds from either (1) the advertising budget for the Chunky brand or (2) profits, thus delaying the accumulation of a profit backlog. Therefore if Chunky were to try to develop either brand (or both) through advertising, it would in some measure compromise the new phase-two objective of consolidation for profits.

---

*$15,356,000—in 2009—AIER

More difficult to assess was the strain on the manufacturing department. Since no new money for machinery could be appropriated, Chunky would have to use present equipment until its own profits had generated an adequate cash reserve. In the meantime the manufacturing department would have to cut costs sharply without spending money for equipment. Since the two manufacturing operations could not be integrated economically, the manufacturing department would have to supervise both plants, and to do so without a significant increase in supervisory personnel. This would strain an implicit corporate objective of trying to get away from continual "crises."

Commenting on the risk involved in the Chunky acquisition, management stated: "There is nothing to lose provided we are careful not to allow the working capital to be depleted below the allowable $244,000. They are willing to change the $300,000 loan to a long-term note, which means we would start off with almost $400,000 in working capital. If we couldn't turn it around before it got down to $244,000, we could simply say, "We're sorry, fellows. We tried our best, but couldn't make it. Now you can have it back."

In another sense there already would be some risk in taking the time and effort away from running our own business. And of course we would be risking our $50,000 down payment.

On February 4, 1958 with time running out, Chunky's management knew that (1) it would have to make its final decision on the basis of existing information (2) the monthly losses being suffered by Schutter were so large that sale of the company would probably be completed in the very near future, it not to Chunky then to another purchaser, and (3) if its offer was accepted, immediate action to eliminate the continuing losses would be needed.

The sale was completed and the action began. It was vital to stop the losses immediately. I employed a management consultant,

Bob Zager, to advise me on the emerging problems sure to arise, and particularly to cope with employee moral as we had to fire 50% of the factory work force, and keep the ones remaining confident of the future of the company.

Sid Luckman was a supplier of some of our packaging materials and a friend. This was the same famous Sid Luckman, the outstanding professional quarterback for the Chicago Bears. He was the first quarterback to use the new T-formation where the quarterback lined up right behind the center. He first became known at Columbia University under the superlative coach Lou Little. Then he became famous with the Chicago Bears of the National Football League. Everyone in Chicago knew Sid and he was exalted for bringing the Chicago Bears a national championship.

I called a meeting of all employees, broken into two groups, one after the other. The first were those who were going to be laid off—about 50%. The second group, the other half, were those who would remain in their jobs.

Sid, a good friend, was happy to stand with me as I spoke to both groups. Although my talk to both groups was basically the same, it was particularly difficult to speak to the first group. I had to offer my sincere regrets that we had to discharge them and I tried to explain the situation as best as I could. It was very clear that "sometimes you had to cut off a finger to save a hand." This would enable us to keep Schutter alive and, operating with Chunky, we could quickly become profitable and, after a short period, hopefully begin rehiring. I told those who were laid off that they would be the first to be brought back. Sid was not only great professional football player, but he was a charismatic speaker as well. He reiterated my views of the desperate Schutter situation. He even told the story of the successful operation of Chunky and how it would bring Schutter to growth, stability, and profits very quickly. In spite of the circumstances, Sid was applauded when he finished.

The anticipated synergism, practical re-organization and rebuilding of the sales operation produced favorable results immediately, and Schutter became profitable in a little over four months. The combined operation continued to grow and become a solid profit center.

CHAPTER 16

A SPONGE-Y MESS

> **Heide Candy Co.**
> **Manhattan, N.Y.**
> **April 1965**

T he Henry Heide Candy Company was founded in 1869 by Henry Heide, an immigrant from Westphalia, Germany. On December 13, 1931, Henry Heide died in New York City. Henry's son, Andrew, began running the business and became the company's fourth president in 1957. He moved the production facility from Hudson Street in New York City to New Brunswick, New Jersey. They manufactured products like Jujyfruits and Jujubes. In addition, they had only one item, Greenfield's Chocolate Sponge, which used chocolate. They wanted to eliminate chocolate from their raw materials and offered to sell Chunky the chocolate sponge product. It easily fit into the Chunky/Schutter operation and offered effective synergism. It would be produced in the Schutter plant in Chicago.

Before we made the payment we made a visit to their plant to see the Sponge machinery operating. To our surprise when we got there, we found that the key machine, which formed the honeycomb "sponge" sections, was covered. Andy Heide, who was a good friend, would not let us see the equipment until after he received payment.

Because of the delicate nature of the product, I arranged for our Brooklyn plant manager, our machinery and equipment engineer, and our Chicago plant manager to study the operation. In addition, I employed the premier Food and Confectionery Laboratory to also be present and to document the manufacturing process. This was a typical belt and suspenders precaution. You can't be too careful. Right!

The operation required very little floor space as the preliminary equipment for handling sugar, corn syrup, and chocolate was already in operation for other products and had available capacity for the "Sponge." The equipment was moved and installed and production was begun.

The first batch started out fine. Except, a few minutes after the honeycomb center was extruded, it collapsed. Okay—no big deal—just be more careful on the next run. Well, careful as we were—and these were experienced, top-flight candy makers—all the batches collapsed. We generated more scrap over the next several days than the entire plant produced in a month. The laboratory technicians, of course, were brought in to make sure we were following the recipe exactly. No help! What to do? Andy Heide could not help. Anyway he wasn't a candy maker anymore than I was.

He did give us the name of the chocolate sponge candy maker who had been in charge of their production and was no longer with them. We finally found him working in the garbage section of the Holiday Inn at 12th Ave and 42nd St. in Manhattan. Our plant manager, offering relatively large amounts of money, couldn't get him to agree to go to Chicago and show us how to process the sponge.

He was afraid of losing his job with the hotel.

Finally I called my friend Bob Tisch, of the famous family which owned Loews Corp. and hotels and insurance companies. He knew the manager of the Holiday Inn and was nice enough to get him to give the candymaker a short leave of absence so he could go to Chicago and show us how to make sponge.

The "sponge" man was a nice person and agreed to go if: (1) we paid him the several thousand dollars in cash in advance, (2) he would have an escort—our assistant Chicago plant manager, (3) he could take his wife with him, and (4) naturally all expenses to be paid.

We agreed. He went. He solved the problem in two batches. The problem was that, in spite of the belt and suspenders, we were mixing the batches incorrectly. It should have been mixed once instead of twice.

A funny way to learn how to make candy!

CHAPTER 17

MORE THAN A FAIR FAIR

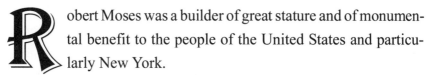

> **Queens, N.Y.**
> **1964-1965**

Robert Moses was a builder of great stature and of monumental benefit to the people of the United States and particularly New York.

He built public works of many kinds—one of the most famous being Jones Beach on the pure, soft white sands of the very wide south shore beach of Long Island.

Another famous accomplishment was the 1964-65 New York World's Fair. He was the major force behind its creation and was its eminently successful CEO. There were many major U.S. and foreign companies that presented expensive exhibits at the Fair.

To cut down on the lead that many marketers of confectionery had because of the much greater length of time they had been in business, I recognized that while it had made considerable strides in its relatively short corporate life, it was still not one of the leaders in the industry. Companies like Hershey, Mars, M & M, and Brach were the industry leaders. Chunky had to demonstrate that it belonged with that elite group. The Fair would serve as a vehicle to do just that.

The consumer exposure which Chunky would receive would be highly valuable. Television advertising competes with other candy advertisers and results are diminished by the "noise level" of competition. The Fair was an opportunity to tell our story without competition from others in the industry. As long as the basic advertising budget was maintained, this "extra" would have a high efficiency return.

The opportunity for sampling Chunky products would be phenomenal. It was estimated that we could sample 5,000,000 persons. We actually sold close to 6,000,000 candy bars.

While we were certainly not in the same class as all the other companies, it gave us recognition and esteem, far beyond our realistic position, with millions of people over a two-year period.

When I first decided to exhibit at the Fair, the inevitable question arose. What would we exhibit, and how would we pay for it? Why couldn't we operate a real candy factory producing one of our candy bars? We designed a production line in two mobile type buildings with a cooling tunnel between. The Greer Company of Massachusetts felt that the exposure would be of significant benefit to them, and were kind enough to donate the cooling tunnel. Erlich, Ben Wilson, Jack Shatz and Curt Frost did Herculean work in putting everything together and making it work.

In addition to the candy factory, I commissioned Oliver O'Connor Barrett, an English artist and sculptor to build a three dimensional Continuum of animals for the exhibit.

Chunky began to plan its participation in the New York World's Fair in the spring of 1963. It was determined after a few months of research that there would be no advantage to Chunky if it were one of the many exhibitors in a large, multi-exhibit pavilion. The potential seemed very limited, inasmuch as Chunky would have been swallowed up by the surrounding major company displays. The cost was astonishingly high—almost $100 per square foot, without taking into consideration the cost of the exhibit itself. The negotiations with the World's Fair Corporation eventually settled for Chunky to have its own 6,000 foot plot. As part of the deal, Chunky negotiated an additional 5,000 feet for landscaping—11,000 square feet in all. Ultimately Chunky was to be one of only 26 prime industrial exhibits at the Fair.

An ambitious exhibit for the site was planned, but one, which when compared to other alternatives, was something which could be done well, without exceeding the carefully calculated budget. The site was to contain three basic elements.

1. A real manufacturing plant, which would automatically chocolate coat, wrap, and package Old Nick candy bars.
2. An area at which products made or distributed by the company could be sold. This would provide a tremendous sampling device, as well as a means to defray some of the cost of the exhibit.
3. An area which was to contain sculptured figures which were both an art form and had a functional use as a children's playground.

The plant, as it was conceived, would be constructed of mobile buildings with glass walls. The equipment in it was to be new and automated. The buildings were built as trailers, hauled to New York on their wheels, fitted out at the Brooklyn plant; and transported to the Fair site by truck. It was an achievement that overcame the tremendous labor cost problems, which almost every exhibitor at the Fair found to be the nemesis of their carefully planned budgets.

The sculpture exhibit, called a "continuum" by its originator and builder, Oliver O'Connor Barrett, consisted of a group of figures, which, when observed through apertures in each unit, fused and became recognizable human, or animal forms. It captured the imagination of art lovers and became one of the leading outdoor activity areas for children.

The selling area sold six-pack and 24 count boxes of Chunkys, Bit O Honey, Kit Kat, and Old Nick at regular retail price. In addition, we also sold 24-pack boxes, as well as a special assortment of 20 candy bars packed in a beautiful souvenir box containing pictures of the Fair and the Chunky exhibit.

The exhibit was budgeted at a net cost to the company of $250,000* as follows:

Expenses:

Rental of space	$ 48,000
Exhibit Costs	$ 370,000
Personnel	$ 50,000
Miscellaneous	$ 40,000
Grand Total:	$ 508,000

Revenues:

Participating Promotion	$ 108,000
Revenue from Sales 60% of $250,000	$ 150,000
	$ 258,000
Net Cost	$ 250,000

---

*$1,729,000 in 2009 dollars—AIER

The actual costs were astonishingly close to the budget, especially in view of the magnitude of this problem with most other exhibitors.

More than 53,000,000 persons paid to visit the World's Fair, which came to a daily average of over 120,000 persons for each of the 365 days the Fair was open. In addition 60,000 employees entered the Fair each day. Attendance at the Chunky pavilion was estimated at 5,600,000, more than 10% of the total paid admission. At times people were packed four and five deep at the factory watching the candy bars being made. What made this especially useful was that almost all the visitors to our exhibit would walk past the entire factory observing each step in the procedure. Most people had never seen a candy factory before and their comments indicated that they were pleased at the cleanliness and the fact that the candy was never directly touched by the personnel. The very latest model enrober, without any superstructure, offered a taste-tempting display of chocolate cascading down and around the candy centers.

The attendance at the major pavilions and the costs as announced follow. Attendance for the pavilions, except Chunky, represents the number of persons who attended the performances that were presented.

Pavilion	Attendance	Estimated Costs*	Cost per Thousand
General Motors	29,002,186	$55,000,000	$1800
The Vatican	27,020,857		
N.Y. State	24,707,204		
Chrysler	18,776,611		
General Electric	15,697,408	$18,000,000	$1100
Ford	14,908,983	$40,000,000	$2800
Florida	14,484,971		
Bell System	12,912,037		
United States	12,000,000		
Spain	10,500,000		
IBM	10,000,000	$22,000,000	$2200
Kodak	7,850,000		
Chunky	5,600,000	$418,000	$74
DuPont	5,256,279		
Johnson Wax	5,050,000		

Sales at the Chunky pavilion amounted to $280,000. The average sale was $ .40, so that 700,000 persons, one in every 8 who visited the pavilion purchased a Chunky product. The public relations benefit was surprisingly good. Descriptions of the exhibit appeared in all major publications from Life magazine to small weeklies and in all the confectionery trade papers. Customers who barely knew what a Chunky was, suddenly read and heard and understood all about it from their local newspapers and radio and TV stations.

One of the best trade relation benefits was the ability to use the Fair as a method to entertain over 1400 out-of-town trade customers.

---

*New York Times—10/19/65

All of these buyers were given VIP tours of the Fair, which enabled them to avoid the long and exasperating lines at major exhibits like GM, Ford, GE, IBM, and Pepsi-Cola.

Our exhibit was everything we hoped it would be when I first set out to make it possible. The only major problem we had not foreseen completely was the drain on corporate energy that the project entailed. All of the top executives of the company were heavily involved in making the Fair exhibit work. Many other projects, which might have contributed to greater corporate profitability, had to be delayed.

Many competitors, suppliers, and customers extended messages of congratulations on the exhibit and evidently thought that it was a significant achievement for the entire industry, as well as for Chunky. Their overall comments, as well as that of many of the articles by the trade press, including one cover story by the leading industry magazine, was that candy was finally presented correctly, in a clean, modern, appetite-appealing manner in an environment of wholesome fun, and that THIS IMAGE, AND THE IMPACT OF THE EXHIBIT, COULD NOT HELP BUT BENEFIT THE ENTIRE CANDY INDUSTRY.

We stayed within our budget, realized the advertising and public relations benefits, and made more than the sales we had planned.

It was a great success!

Thank you, Robert Moses.

UNE 2, 1964

Ninetieth Year

CHUNKY ADVANCES SCIENCE OF BAR PRODUCTION AT THE WORLD'S FAIR

Chunky Exhibit—New York World's Fair—1964-65

Jaffe with sculptor Oliver O'Connor Barrett
and the famous Robert Moses

Hal Hansen and Jaffe

Sonny Nelson

Jim Spiegel

Virginia Tech Corps of Cadets. Jaffe Eager Squad Winners—2007

Jeff and Natalie
Luxemborg Gardens
Paris 1990

Marjorie Jaffe Sklar

Jeff, Dick Cash, Sylvan Stein
Long Island, N.Y.—1972

CHAPTER 18

EXCEPT WHEN IT ISN'T!

**Dean Street
Brooklyn, NY
February 22, 1967**

hough it was winter, there was no hint of snow, or the dark and ominous cloud of disaster that was soon to appear.

During the half-hour drive to my office on the fifth floor of the Chunky Chocolate factory in Brooklyn, my thoughts dwelled on the excellent progress my company was making with both the CHUNKY chocolate bar and the BIT-O-HONEY candy bar. Sales were continuing to grow and profits were better than ever.

There were offers to buy Chunky by General Mills, and others, and all were turned down. The situation was perfect for me. It meant a total ownership of a company that was achieving national distribution of a candy bar, two small but efficient factories and making profits with a brand, clearly becoming a strong national brand as well as an existing one. Nothing could happen which would weaken the company! I was feeling in great spirits that morning, feeling that nothing could possibly go wrong now.

It was only ten minutes later that my world came crashing down.

I was just taking off my coat and about to sit down at my desk when Manny Goldstein, the financial vice-president rushed in. He was breathless and from the look in his eye, apparently frightened of something.

"The Food and Drug Administration is demanding we recall all Chunky products."

I sat there, completely amazed.

Goldstein continued to report. "They had inspected the plant two weeks before and discovered Salmonella at our plant."

For a moment, I thought Goldstein would collapse. After taking a glass of water he explained further. "You see, Jeff, they were following up on a shipment from the Blumenthal Chocolate Co. in Philadelphia contained traces of salmonella and which were probably present in CHUNKY bars."

This perfect day had changed into a major catastrophe.

"What the hell is salmonella? I shouted. In my desire to get to the heart of the matter, I had several of the production managers in my office and began asking a series of questions. "How did we get it? When they took samples did we take matching samples? Was this announced publicly in the office or the plant?"

I began to piece everything together. The FDA detected salmonella in a dairy and traced the milk shipment to the Blumenthal Chocolate Company in Philadelphia. When questioned, Blumenthal said that the milk in question was used in the milk chocolate that was shipped to the Chunky Chocolate Company in Brooklyn, NY. The FDA then took several dozen samples of Chunkys. Chunky took the same samples at the same time. The FDA tests claimed that there were traces of salmonella in 3 samples. The Chunky samples, tested at a registered independent laboratory, showed zero contamination

In the ensuing weeks the Food and Drug Administration demanded a total recall of all Chunky products, including PECAN CHUNKYS, even though that bar was made with a different chocolate than the original CHUNKY.

Salmonella is a very common bacterium. It can be found in your breakfast eggs, or in any food, or on your cutting board in the kitchen. It comes from cows or birds and has been ingested by the human race from time immemorial. It is generally harmless although it can cause illness in infants or weakened elderly persons. I discovered that that particular shipment of chocolate under suspicion had been fully used up many weeks before, and the CHUNKY product had been consumed by many people without any ill effect. But I soon discovered that trying to wipe away bad news with the good was a futile experience.

After Tom Brokaw announced the Chunky recall on the NBC National TV evening news we received about 35 or 40 letters seeking money. No claimant ever offered proof of any illness, nor did any claimant ever follow up their original letter. No settlement, payment or any consideration ever had to be made by the Chunky Company. We tried to explain our predicament to the FDA, hoping they would understand.

But the FDA was adamant, It resisted all appeals and demanded a complete recall and a supervised destruction of the product. When we asked what would happen if the company refused to recall all the product, the FDA advised that federal marshals would be delegated to handle the recall, and that I could face a jail sentence. Our company had retained a law firm that specialized in FDA cases. They confirmed that possibility.

Whether from whimsy or malice, ego or budget enhancement, their motivation is difficult to understand. It was first encounter with the bureaucracy that existed in Washington.

The nights spent trying to sort this problem into something that would ensure Chunky's existence was my worst nightmare. I felt like I had been punched in the stomach. After talking with the lawyers, I felt as if I was kicked in the groin. Heart-rending is the only way to describe the sensation I felt as I watched Tom Brokaw announce a total recall of Chunky Chocolate bars. It is usually possible to work out problems with time, money, energy or brains. Problems created by others are sometime resolvable by negotiation.

With the FDA there is no negotiating, no discussion of the problem, and no interest on their part to see the problem they had created. I met with the then New York director at Bush Terminal in Brooklyn, NY. I remember clearly that at first I could not even remember my phone number when I tried to call the office. I was in shock, pure and simple.

For a meeting in Washington, which I requested, I hired a legal firm that reputedly had often worked with the FDA. When we explained that Pecan Chunky's were made with completely different chocolate than regular Chunkys, and the FDA had no cause or evidence to demand a total recall of all Chunky products, it fell on deaf ears.

But in the industry there was major shock. Nothing like this had ever happened before. The agony of every one involved at Chunky was reflected by the industry. What would happen next? Nine months later Mars, the giant in the candy industry, was found to have salmonella in their M&M product. In that case the FDA allowed them to recall only one batch of their M&M production. Why, I wondered, would they permit M&M to continue production while completely stopping Chunky?

The recall put Chunky in a technical state of bankruptcy. It also wiped out my personal net worth. My wife, Natalie, clearly understood this and was marvelous in her support and help during the difficult times. She had a thorough understanding of the business as well as financial markets. She was always fully supportive of Chunky since the beginning when she operated the Sugar Toasted Peanut bagging machine preliminary to our scheduling a night shift.

Now what? Talk about problems, talk about crisis. How would we survive? What options were available?

Well, first we had to recall all Chunkys from all customers at our cost. Then it all had to be destroyed under the visual inspection of the government. What little funds we had took care of that. All accounts receivable were frozen, never to be paid.

Then we had to "sanitize" the plant. Tests taken all over the plant and equipment, showed no salmonella anywhere. But we still had to demonstrate compliance with the sanitization procedure and satisfy the FDA (I now refer to it as the F-FDA.)

In 1967 during the devastating trauma of the Chunky product recall, Rowntree sent two engineers to examine the Chunky plant. I don't know what they were expected to do, but apparently the executives in York, England, assumed that the salmonella problem was caused by some fault in the Chunky manufacturing operation. Everyone else knew the problem was caused by tainted chocolate being shipped to Chunky. It also made me question the entire episode. Why, for example, was the Blumenthal Chocolate Company, the manufacturers of the very chocolate which contained Salmonella permitted to continue production without any recall? In any event, Rowntree treated Chunky as if it was sick. It unceremoniously dropped Chunky as the importer and marketer of Kit-Kat in the US. The action of Rowntree in terminating this working partnership with Chunky, after Chunky performed so well in achieving national distribution for Kit-Kat was obviously a BETRAYAL of the Quaker virtues of which they were so proud. In the 19th Century in England the three large Quaker owned chocolate and confectionery companies—Cadbury, Rowntree and Fry—zealously followed the virtues that their faith was built upon. In fact, they provided many benevolent services for the community and the local residents which actually took priority over practical business considerations.* However, in the 20th Century no one was expected to operate a business following high moral philosophies as espoused by the Quakers, even if they were Quakers. Nonetheless, for Rowntree to abruptly discontinue its association with Chunky after we had performed so well, was a BETRAYAL. Even though there was no written contract, the association between Rowntree and Chunky was, or should have been, as good as a written contract, which was similar to many in the candy and other industries. It also was, from a practical business point of view, a missed opportunity of great magnitude which, most certainly, would have resulted in Rowntree owning a significant confectionery company in the United States. The acquisitions, developments, growth and profits which I and my associates achieved with Ward Foods (see Chapter 19) would surely have been exceeded by a continued association with Rowntree. The profits would have been exponentially greater than the relatively minor royalties received from Hershey had Rowntree had the vision and fortitude to make a deal with Chunky. Chunky had willingly invested significant assets in marketing Kit-Kat in the U.S. There was a great amount of corporate energy, time, executive travel, sales management and the use of a proven national

---

*Chocolate Wars by Deborah Cadbury

sales force, use of cash, ongoing customer contacts, office administration, advertising planning, and knowledge of U.S. marketing, warehousing, shipping, and collecting receivables, all of which would have cost Rowntree a great amount of money and time had they set up an organization to do it themselves.

It never crossed my mind that the "permanent agreement" we had with Rowntree would ever end except for actual poor performance which obviously was not the case. We were successful beyond the goals that were agreed upon by both companies.

The abrupt termination ended the possibility of forthcoming future profits so diligently earned by Chunky's success with Kit-Kat. The lavish investments it had made with the goal of ongoing profits in the future were totally WASTED.

"I would like to be bitter but there is no time to be bitter."

-Nelson Mandela

Former President of South Africa

If all of this had been used for Chunky, it would have advanced our company a lot further and a lot faster.

Some years before, Lloyd Owen, Rowntree's Chairman, made an offer to buy 10% of Chunky. I declined, as I knew that at that early stage, the value was miniscule compared to what it would eventually be worth. Even after the disastrous recall, the sale to Ward Foods proved that to be true.

At the time of Rowntree's first contact with us, England was just emerging from the trauma due to the privations and sacrifices which the British so courageously endured throughout World War II.

Robert Fitzgerald, School of Management, University of London wrote ROWNTREE AND THE MARKETING REVOLUTION, which was published in 1995. It is a brilliant, lengthy and totally inclusive erudite history of Rowntree from 1862-1969. Inclusive, that is, except that Chunky is merely mentioned once as "Rowntree, in 1963, investigated the possibility of joint manufacturing and marketing with the Chunky Chocolate Corporation." It totally ignores the 15 years 1952-1967 wherein Chunky achieved national distribution and significant sales of Kit-Kat in the U.S. It reveals that Rowntree first became interested in expanding into the US. in 1920. Their efforts during all those years were timid and feeble.

Lloyd Owen, Rowntree's Chairman, died unexpectedly in 1966. Had he survived through the disastrous Chunky recall of 1967, he would probably have made an offer to buy all or part of Chunky. At that time it would have been successful. The management of Rowntree, then under Chairman Donald Barron, completely ignored the opportunity. "In 1970 Rowntree sold its U.S. Kit-Kat rights to Hershey, some financial returns from negotiations being better than no return at all." This was Rowntree's own rationalization. Actually the Hershey deal benefited me as, by that time, I had acquired a substantial amount of Hershey stock.

During the 15 years of our association, I met and worked with at least a dozen Rowntree executives. With rare exceptions, each one was wise, highly competent, and supremely dedicated to his responsibility. They had the ability to think!

Ralph Kaner, who became Chairman of the United Kingdom Confectionery Division in 1985, was typical. When he was about to speak or answer a question he would first pause, then touch his chin and then expound on the subject, articulating in perfect sentences, his words sounding logical and well-reasoned. He was one of the smartest with a lightening fast mind, and remains a friend today. I was always impressed with the group, but maybe it was because of the mellifluous tones of their English accent.

Kaner's responsibility included 20,000 employees producing £500,000,000 ($637,000,000) of revenue. This included all confectionery sales of Rowntree, Mackintosh and others in the United Kingdom. There were manufacturing plants in York, Newcastle, Halifax, Leicester, Castleford, Norwich, and Edinburgh.

Often we would host visitors from various Rowntree operations around the world. In the early 60's I hosted one of their top executives from their German factory. It turned out that he was a former U-boat Captain, which was a little difficult for us at first. But he was an engaging fellow and we were able to forget past history. He thought running my 42-foot cabin cruiser was great fun and we all had a delightful time.

One who gains strength by overcoming obstacles possesses the only strength which can overcome adversity.
Dr. Albert Schweitzer—Nobel Peace Prize Winner

CHAPTER 19

WHAT'S NEXT?

655 Dean Street
Brooklyn, N.Y.
March, 1967

W here do we turn?

No money, no accounts receivable, salaries to pay, a skeleton plant, raw and packaging materials needed.

Can we get back into business?

Well the Schutter operation was thriving and would continue to generate revenue and cash.

We could build on that!

I contacted a number of companies in an effort to make some kind of a deal that would enable me to revive a growing and profitable Chunky business.

Making those phone calls made me realize I was considered a plague in the industry. Most companies contacted would not even agree to a meeting to discussed the situation. The one ray of light was with Chuck Call of Ward Foods. Chuck was affiliated with the old Ward Baking Co. Five years before, Charlie Bluhdorn of Gulf & Western Industries invested $3,000,000* with Call who was then a financial advisor.

Chuck took the entire $3,000,000 and bought the Ward Baking Co. and immediately pushed the unprofitable white bread bakeries onto the back burner.

Chuck and the Board of Directors quickly decided that dependence on just one product was not only unwise but dangerous. At the time of that purchase, Ward Baking was an all-your-eggs-in-one-basket operation. It was a poor way to run a company, especially one that had always shown little or no potential.

Diversification was the obvious answer, but only in food and food related items. For the most part, horizontal expansion was logical but when appropriate, Ward could consider some vertical movement as well.

Certainly nothing new, but very, very sound.

Stop the losses, broaden the financial base, and begin an acquisition program. What occurred was an incredible thirty-two acquisitions in only nine years. Here are just a few of those acquisitions:

1963—Jersey Farm & Farm Crest Bakeries
1964—Rose Royal Cheese Cake Co
       Nancy Alice Pie Company.
       Jersey Farm, San Francisco
       American Sheep Co. (Gold Ring Meats).
1965—Honey Crust Donut Corp

---

*$19,258,000—2009 Dollars—AIER

1966—Honolulu Iron Works:
      Honiron—Philippines
      J & L Engineering
      G.M. Industries
      Russell-Phinney Pies, Inc.
      Protein Products

I joined Ward Foods in 1967 and became President and Chief Operating Officer (COO) shortly thereafter.

1967—Schutter Candy Co.
      Simple Simon Frozen Pies
      Continental Seafoods, Inc.
      (Tweedy Holdings) Limited
1968—Food Corp. of America:
      Plymouth Rock Provision Co.
      Wisconsin Foods, Inc.
      Holsum (Hawaii) Baking, Inc.
      Zuider Zee Oyster Bar, Inc.:
            Great Southwest Wholesale Fish & Oyster Co.
      The Chunky Corp.
      Color-Ad Packaging, Inc.
      Meadow Maid Donut Co., Inc.
      Marigold Foods, Inc.
      Bilich Oyster Co.
      Quality Col-Pak, Inc.:
            Bert Lane Distributors
            California Apple Products

1969—Blumenthal Bros. Chocolate Co.

F & L Bakers, Inc.

Tijuana Taco, Inc.

Robert A. Johnston Co., Inc.

Atarraya, S.A.

Manufacturera 3M

1970—Superior Potato Chips, Inc.

1971—Williamson Candy Co.

Quinlan Pretzel Co.

Reading Pretzel Machinery Corp.

Being CEO of all these companies might seem to be difficult and complicated. But it was neither. There were many synergies available and being "one boss" allowed a great amount of flexibility, goal setting and control. Of course, having good managers in place or employing them was vital to the success.

In the years from 1963 to 1971 the net worth of Ward Baking went from $23,916,000 to $46,536,000.*

Sales jumped from $156,520,000 to $414,523,000.

Net Income went from a loss of $3,235,000 to a profit of $2,138,000 in 2009 dollars.

Chuck Call was not a small man. He was six feet four inches in his stockings and weighed well over 250 pounds. But he was all good humor and had a razor sharp mind. The power of his physical presence, the power of his personality and most of all the power of his financial mind all contributed to his compelling leadership. In spite of that he was humble with a self-negating, innocent approach.

---

* $246,175,440—AIER

He would often jot some numbers on the back of an envelope and go to the Chase Bank and borrow another several million dollars to purchase the next acquisition which he and I were making.

He fell in love with Chunky and Schutter and made a deal wherein I got an appreciable amount of money without undue risk to Ward.

Before the catastrophic recall I had promised Al Erlich a 15% interest in the company. I was happy to fulfill that commitment at the time of the Ward deal, and at Erlich's untimely death, some years later, I bought back the equity for its increased value.

Chunky, with Ward's credit behind it, was able to resume operations and never used one penny of money from Ward Foods.

Ward Foods consisted of seven operating groups engaged in the food business. The candy, chocolate, and dessert group accounted for 32% of Ward's sales in 1976 and soon became the largest profit center of the company. Production and distribution of bar and boxed candy, chocolate coatings, cocoa powder, and frozen desserts, were the principal activities of this group.

Candy was sold under trademarks Chunky, Oh Henry, Bit-O-Honey, Sno-Caps, Goobers and Raisinets. Boxed candy was sold under the Surrey label and was distributed primarily through charities and service organizations.

Candy and dessert products were produced in eight manufacturing facilities employing approximately 1,800 persons.

Chuck Call was first and always a financial planner. As Ward continued to grow, operations became too much for Chuck and he asked me to become President and COO of Ward Foods. Although I was reluctant to leave my secure, profitable and esteemed candy and chocolate companies, Ward presented an irresistible opportunity to be responsible for the multi-faceted operations of what was soon to be a half-billion dollar public company. I relished the challenge and became President and COO of Ward Foods.

The widely diverse companies of Ward were each headed by a successful entrepreneur. An important element of the new President COO's job was to provide a climate in which they could operate independently and maximize their skills and leadership. At the same time it was important that each unit satisfy the goals and corporate procedures upon which we mutually agreed.

This required a different type of leadership, communication and relationship than directly operating a specific company. Entrepreneurs are forever entrepreneurs. The very qualities that make them successful in building and operating their own companies result in difficulties when they have sold.

This was what had happened to me. I was no longer able to run my very own company because of an incident beyond my control. But I still had to accept that reality. Instead of operating my own team I had to become part of another team. It took some serious thinking and was ultimately resolved satisfactorily. With rare exceptions, the transition with the other company CEO's was equally satisfactory.

Companies that are listed on the New York Stock Exchange, as was Ward Foods, usually make presentations to financial analysts, bankers and research advisers. As President of Ward, I planned, scheduled and hosted such a meeting with a luncheon in the Time-Life private dining room on Sixth Avenue in Manhattan.

It was a great opportunity to explain the company to about forty-five financial executives who attended the luncheon. Welcoming them, I called their attention to the luncheon menu at each place. It read:

Shrimp Cocktail
Roast Beef and Lamb Chops
Potato Chips
Bread and Rolls
Chocolate Ice Cream
Apple Pie
Assorted Chocolate Candies

One method used to emphasize something special is a three-step dialogue, which goes like this:

<u>Our Version</u>

1. "First I'm gonna tell you what I'm gonna tell you. Opening Menu

2. "Then I'm gonna tell you Lunch

3. "And then I'm gonna tell you what I told you Menu identifying Ward products made by Ward companies

After dessert, and before the financial presentation, a second menu was given to each person. It read:

Shrimp Cocktail	Continental Seafood—New York
Roast Beef and Lamb Chops	Gold Ring Beef, LA & Plymouth Rock N.Y.
Potato Chips	Superior Potato Chip Co.—PA.
Bread and Rolls	Ward Baking
Chocolate Ice Cream	Marigold Foods, Minneapolis
Apple Pie	Johnson Frozen Pie, Los Angeles
Assorted Chocolate Candies	Ward Candy Co. N.Y.

This was greeted with many surprised voices offering praise and commendation for our dramatic way of showing and sampling the span and potential of Ward Foods.

Then Chuck Call, our Chairman & CEO, made a very charismatic presentation of our recent financial history and current goals. Without exception, the group gave us high marks and left with an optimistic financial view of Ward Foods.

CHAPTER 20

OOPS

April, 1960
Louisville, Kentucky

The Klotz Candy Company, in Louisville Kentucky, manufactured fudge bars and peanut brittle. Like Bit-O-Honey there was a lot of synergism possible if we owned it. It was an efficient operation, without any need to add non-manufacturing personnel to the organization.

Although it was not a large operation, it seemed to be a good prospect to add to our bottom line. So I bought it.

But after three years we closed it down. Apparently there was a lack of interest on the part of customers as we tried to expand its regional base to national distribution. The product had a short shelf life, and lots of regional competitive products.

Although we made a little money, it did not quite cover what we paid for the business.

I was a klutz with Klotz!

CHAPTER 21

ANOTHER KIND OF HOME RUN

June, 1971
Cicero Avenue
Chicago, Ill

About a mile and a half east of the Schutter factory on Cicero Ave., was the Williamson Candy Co. It was started by a genial, down-to-earth Scotsman named George Williamson. His main product was the famous Oh-Henry candy bar. This was a chocolate covered nut roll with nougat and caramel.

This was well before Henry Aaron was born, and the name of the candy bar had nothing to do with Hank. (Of course it was Hank Aaron who ultimately broke Babe Ruth's long standing life-time home run record.)

It is fascinating to recall that there was, and still is, another nut roll. It was called Baby Ruth. Similarly, this name had nothing to do with the famous ball player, but was named after the child of one of the owners of the Curtis Candy Co. Although the two candy bars were similar, Baby Ruth was coated with imitation chocolate and Oh Henry used genuine chocolate.

It cost us more, but the difference in taste was significant, and we decided to maintain the genuine ingredients. We felt that the higher cost was more than compensated for by a real competitive advantage.

The negotiations were very amicable and proceeded smoothly. George was quite old and was anxious to sell his company and retire. By that time, as part of Ward Foods, I was able to assemble the purchase price without any problem.

Why was it a home run?

SYNERGISM

It was flawlessly perfect. The Williamson Sales Department - discontinued. The office and administrative departments discontinued. The entire factory - shut down and the building was sold. The manufacturing facilities at Schutter had both the capability and capacity to produce all of the Oh Henry candy bars. Of course it was unfortunate that we had to discharge most of the Williamson personnel, but the savings were tremendous. It took about eight months to complete the merger and it provided a tremendous increase in our profits.

We actually used Aaron in our advertising for Oh Henry!

CHAPTER 22

SCHRAFFTS

> **March 1973**
> **Gulf & Western Bldg.**
> **Columbus Circle**
> **Manhattan, NY**

In 1973 I was 53 years old, in retirement, but eager to go back to work. Ward Foods had been sold. There was no room for me with the new owners. One day I got a call from Charlie Bluhdorn, who was the charismatic, iconic CEO of Gulf & Western Industries. It was Bluhdorn who financed the purchase of Ward Foods (formerly Ward Baking Co,) and installed Chuck Call, a financial advisor, as CEO. Charlie had brains, guts and an overflowing level of hubris. His plush offices in the Gulf & Western building overlooking Central Park in Manhattan were exactly in the form and style that a dramatic film director might design. When I was ushered into his office, he was talking on three telephones—New York, London and the Dominican Republic. There were two secretaries shuttling in and out while he was talking. It was the kind of scene you wouldn't believe unless you saw it in a movie. Only this was no movie. It was real.

Schrafft Factory—Charlestown, Mass.

He told me he wanted to buy the Schrafft Company Co. and wanted me to run it.

I asked him why he would want Schraffts at all since he was really engaged in major industrial businesses he already had acquired. He said there were two reasons. First, he wanted to build a consumer business around Consolidated Cigar which he already owned. Secondly, Schraffts would come with a negative good will of $19,000,000.* Even for Gulf & Western this was not an insignificant sum in 1973 and it could immediately be booked as profit.

He said he wanted me to be Vice President of a Consumer Products Division, reporting to the President of that division. I said that was okay provided that I was in complete charge of Schrafft without interference. He asked me if I could turn the Schrafft losses into a profit and if so, how long would it take. I said twelve months. He agreed. (It actually took six months).

---

*$91,751,000—2009 Dollars—AIER

Schraffts was a candy and chocolate company based in Sullivan Square, Charlestown, Mass. The famous Schrafft's neon sign was a significant landmark in Boston. William F. Schrafft founded the candy company in 1861.

The Schrafft factory consisted of over 750,000 sq ft in a six story building filled with machinery and its own power plant, and employed over 1000 workers. It manufactured almost every kind of candy imaginable which was really the main problem. Having an abundance of candies meant having to produce losers along with the winners. But the losers generated losses. I immediately cut out about 200 s.k.u.'s (stock keeping units) which were totally unprofitable. This was about a third of the total, and reduced the sales volume from $40,000,000 to $32,000.000. I also divided the sales department into three sections.

I was fortunate that I was able to get Ben Wilson to be my manufacturing vice president. He had been with me at Chunky and Schutter and was highly competent, energetic, and dedicated. Ben, from a German background of several generations, was stubborn, willful, but always fully discharged his responsibilities. He was contentious, but once a decision was made, faithfully followed through. He was a wonderful man and we had great mutual respect and liking for each other.

Equally fortunate was having George Rausch join us. He was a bright-eyed, bright-minded executive from another candy company. Our thinking was generally very similar, but he was never hesitant about disagreeing with me and pointing out better reasoning for a better result. He participated with me in many decisions and eventually became Executive Vice President. He was, and still is, a good friend.

The Schrafft factory was a major installation with the capability of manufacturing any and every type of candy. It even had its own candy box manufacturing department. Among the many types of packages the Schrafft's manufacturing department produced was the fancy "extended edge" package. This was the box used to market the high-priced, assorted quality chocolates at that time.

My very first action after I became CEO was to scrap the ill-assorted, ancient, uncomfortable rickety chairs in the company cafeteria. I replaced them with comfortable, bright orange plastic chairs. The cafeteria was large enough to serve most of the employees at the same time. Not only was the appearance most attractive, but the spirit of the employees rocketed to a high. I always walked through a different part of the factory every day and the employees were vocal in their appreciation of the concern for their well-being. For years no one had paid any attention to them. They knew that the company was losing a lot of money and were worried about their jobs. This concern for them immediately resulted in their conviction that we came to effect a turnaround and operate it profitably, and not skim off the assets in the hope of selling the valuable real estate.

During the ensuing years my consideration for the employees was always a top priority.

For six months I never heard a word from my boss, the President of Gulf & Western Consumer Products. I sent in my reports every month, first a "flash" on the last day of the month followed by the official monthly financial report. When my reports started showing a profit, he visited me and began making noises about combining purchasing and sales with the cigar company. I categorically refused to even discuss the matter. This didn't help our relationship, which actually was terrible from our very first meeting.

Ben Wilson did an outstanding job running the factory. The factory hummed with a rhythm that made for efficiency. Ben had a strong ability to get the most production out of factory personnel. More important, he also had an instinct of knowing when someone was falling down on the job. As efficiency improved and production increased significantly, the business began turning a profit. Ben's crew was able to pack as much as 90,000 pounds of fine assorted chocolates—32 pieces to the pound—in a single day. Of course we did not manufacture all of this on the same day. Different pieces were made in advance. We also sold millions of dollars of larger candies. These were packed at 18 pieces to the pound. Such candies were sold to the large mass merchandisers such as Wal-Mart, Kmart, and Sears. We managed to do all this while producing dozens of other types of candies in large quantities.

Schrafft's other factory was in Reading, Pennsylvania which happened to be the area center for many factory discount stores. These stores were successful beyond belief, operated by companies which sold clothing, hardware, food, lingerie, make-up, books and a number of other items.

Every day busses drove in from surrounding areas filled with eager buyers anxious to take advantage of the discounted prices.

Schraffts 250,000 sq.ft. plant had an excellent location contiguous to the area, and there was ample ground floor room to set up a retail store. I opened a store there in 1977. It was a highly profitable bonanza. Sales the first year exceeded $1,000,000* and led to opening other candy outlet stores in locations shared with Gulf & Western Companies.

---

*$3,538,000 in 2009 dollars—AIER

I was delighted with my job at Schraffts. While I was never satisfied to work for a large corporation, Charlie Bluhdorn had convinced me with "an offer I couldn't refuse." At the end of the five-year contract I had signed, it was mutually agreed to end our association.

Working for Gulf & Western had an interesting perk. Charlie Bluhdorn was then head of Paramount Pictures and as Natalie and I happened to be in France at the time of the Cannes Film Festival, he arranged for us to be guests at the Festival. It was exciting for us. We had dinner at the same table with Donald O'Connor and his wife and David Carradine and his friend. At the next table Fred Astaire and Gene Kelley were enjoying the evening as much as we. Some of the movie actors assumed that, because we were with G & W, we were involved in the movie industry with Paramount and came over to us and introduced themselves. I didn't disabuse them with the facts.

At that time Paramount was issuing a remake of King Kong. Charlie called me and said, between his numerous phone calls and letters written by secretaries, that he wanted to have a King Kong candy bar. A King Kong bar. I tried to realize what that might look like. I knew it was senseless to argue. It was well known that whatever Charlie wants Charlie gets. So we created a King Kong Bar to his liking, which was easy. The King Kong Bar was a chocolate-covered peanut butter crunch bar—an excellent product and Charlie was able to exploit the movie with it.

I was proud of the achievements. Taking a company with a big loss and turning it into a substantial profit was good, and equally important was leaving a manufacturing facility which was greatly improved and able to compete with the best in the industry. Equally important, it was a company where the employee morale and spirit was at a very high level.

Schrafft Candy Honored For Advertising Excellence

The Schrafft Candy Company is the 1975 winner of the "Andy" Merit Award for advertising excellence. The award is given annually by the New York Advertising Club and includes entries from all over the country and all categories of merchandise.

Above, sharing the honors for the award are Jeff Jaffe, president of Schrafft and Warren Pfaff, president of Warren Pfaff, Inc., Schrafft's advertising agency.

The winning entry was a radio campaign featuring an original song entitled "Have We Got a Candy For You."

CHAPTER 23

HARVARD BUSINESS SCHOOL

September 15, 1960
655 Dean Street,
Brooklyn, NY

"Roland Christiansen calling," the phone surprisingly announced that fall morning. Chris was a senior professor at the Harvard Business School. At that time it was considered the best business school in the country.

I grabbed the phone, delighted to hear from a new friend whom I greatly admired. I had taken the shortened Advanced Management Program course at Harvard as part of the Young President's Organization activities. Having been schooled as an engineer, I felt fortunate in being exposed to the case studies, classes and lectures which Chris presented.

I could not imagine why Chris was calling me since the AMP course had been completed months before. I was flattered when he said that he wanted to set up a case study series on my company. Why us? I asked. What could we offer to students of advanced management, most from America's largest and most successful companies? He explained that they were interested in the activities of the General Manager. In this case me as CEO. What were the relationships between me and my various subordinates, good and bad? What was the state of communications, delegations, negotiations and responsibility? Chunky offered this opportunity. I was dubious that this group of successful prime executives could learn much, if anything, from us, but the thought of participating in something with the Harvard Business School was intriguing. I agreed and we set up a plan whereby Bruce Scott, then his research assistant, would do the research and case writing. What followed is history-summarized by an article in the Harvard Business School Bulletin.

It was published in May 1977.

HONORS FOR THE "MIDWAY" CASE SERIES
By Wanda A. Lankenner

Three men are honored for their work on the "Midway" cases, one of the school's most comprehensive and successful series.

More than 10,000 Harvard Business School students—MBAs, AMPs, and PMDs alike—have sharpened their business wits on the " Midway" case series. Its form and emphasis constitute a landmark in case writing. Midway is one of the Business School's most successful teaching materials. It is essentially the work of three men— Jeff Jaffe, whose willingness in 1957 to disclose his company's workings supplied the material; Professor C. Roland Christiansen, who oversaw the investigation and case writing; and Professor Bruce Scott, then a Research Assistant, who gathered and wrote up the data. In a ceremony on December 9th at the home of Dean Fouraker, these men were honored. The event furnished an opportunity to reward both a cooperative manager and the faculty members who transformed his situation into a long-lived teaching tool.

The ceremony itself was characterized by that special appreciation the School shows its benefactors. During a surprise cocktail party to mark the occasion, Dean Fouraker presented commemorative plaques to both Jaffe and Scott. Professor Christiansen, unable to attend, received his award the following day. In expressing the School's gratitude to Jaffe, Dean Fouraker remarked: "Midway is well thought out and was fully supported by its company. Cases like it are at the core of the educational process at Harvard. It has relevance to the professional manager in all his endeavors." The plaque Jaffe received, a facsimile of a casebook, read: PRESENTED TO JEFF JAFFE IN APPRECIATION FOR HIS IMPORTANT SERVICE TO THE HARVARD BUSINESS SCHOOL.

Successive classes have given Midway new currency. The series began in the classroom as well. In 1957, Professor Christensen taught Jeff Jaffe in a Young Presidents' Organization seminar. Noticing then that Jaffe was "an intellectually curious pragmatic businessman of the highest integrity," Christensen and Jaffe evolved the idea of submitting Chunky Candy Corp. (which Jaffe then owned) to a casewriter's scrutiny. Christensen judged the company worth investigating. At the same time, the company's situation, in Christensen's opinion could meet a perceived need "to do a better job at merging administrative practices and business policies in case writing." Administrative practice was considered "People without substance" and business policy, "Substance without people." We wanted to highlight both the human and the technical dimensions. Especially, we wanted to show the human interaction on all levels as well as its process and its power.

Professor Scott was chosen to interview and write. "I invested half my time for a year in the interviewing." Scott recalled. "What was unique was management's willingness to cooperate in revealing itself. I stayed for a week at a time with four of the principal executives. I talked with their wives and even their children. Previous cases had put the company and the social system together in a 25-page package. This was different."

The difference emerged as a case series unique in length, format, and emphasis. The Midway material is presented as a long series building toward the final two cases. These two cases dealt particularly with the job of the general manager. It is a complex reconstruction of the history of a company over several years based on incidents that deal with the functional and human problems arising in the management of an enterprise that suffers adversity and enjoys success.

Professor Christiansen described the format's crystallization. "Bruce Scott and I were in my upstairs study at home. We drew four circles. That was the Midway case. The A case was the environment—industry opportunities, competitive characteristics, company resources, major company goals. In the C case we wanted functional departments—their mission, methods of operation, operating problems, and the philosophy of the executives responsible for each department. We then wanted issues that would cut across these departments—that's the D series. But we had a missing link. It wasn't enough to introduce environment, strategy, and issues. We had to introduce the mood, the value system, too. That's B. It highlights the entrepreneurial character of the company."

If B highlights the company's entrepreneurial style, the last two cases, known as E, highlight Jaffe himself, the entrepreneur—his role in directing and coordinating operations, his interactions with individual executives, and his idea of himself. "We made a bigger investment in the social system than we ever had before," Professor Scott noted. "E is a character study of the president in his relationship to the company and the outside world. It's an intimate portrait.

"Chris and I were stressing," Scott continued, "that what was needed in business policy was a more profound understanding of the social system before making administrative recommendations. That was a big gain in separating economic and technical information from data on the social system.

"We added further depth to the series with the H case, written about five years later. It describes the stresses in the social system during a severe economic setback, and then the breakup of the group, which had built the company up to that point. It helps develop a deeper appreciation of the personal impact of a chief executive on his organization. The ultimate fascination of the cases is analyzing the strengths and weaknesses of the president and how this mix influences the functioning of the company's social system and ultimately its economic fortune as well."

Cases in the Midway series are used by nearly 1,000 MBA students and participants in Executive Education Programs at the Business School each year. Nearly 5,000 sets have been used by other universities in the past seven years. Since the publication of the series in 1969 approximately 50 U.S. academic institutions have purchased Midway cases from the Intercollegiate Case Clearing House. They include institutions as diverse and far-flung as the University of Puerto Rico, Northwestern University, the University of Hawaii, Stanford University, Syracuse University, Ohio University, and the University of Kansas. Foreign schools using the series have included York University, the Ecole des Hautes Etudes, the University of Glasglow, and the London School of Business. Business associations and consulting groups have also found the series valuable: General Motors, IBM, General Electric, Morgan Guaranty Trust, the Asiatic Petroleum Corporation, the National Confectioners' Association, the Society of Industrial Accountants of Canada, and Arthur D. Little, Inc. have all used the Midway cases as part of their in-house educational programs.

Jeff Jaffe, now president of the Schrafft Candy Company, has returned to the Business School each year since 1960 to discuss Midway with AMP classes. His performance underscores the educational value of one man's energy and honesty. His satisfaction is a personal one. Jeff is given the chance to explain his success, his difficulties and his wisdom. Jaffe says of the experience: "It has all been a tremendous pleasure. What started as an accident is fun. I enjoy my involvement and look forward to it."

Professor Theodore Levitt, who has taught Midway to AMPs and PMDs, agrees. "Jaffe has always enjoyed coming, always been pleased. I think he gets great satisfaction in being in front of that class. He's not fazed in the least. He ends up winning because the classes always respond well. They push him, he takes it, comes back with clarity and without apology. He will admit to error and uncertainty. He enjoys encountering people at all levels—we have to drag him away from the students. He's making a continuing contribution."

To Christiansen and Scott, Midway presented an opportunity to change the face of teaching form. "Sometimes we didn't know what the case was going to be," Christensen confesses. "Once you win the ballgame, though, it's easy to talk about. We designed a new form, a form that moved away from the traditional historical presentations to a multiple-case format. We did this by looking at the data until their special uniformities emerged." A uniformity to note is Scott's part of the cases' unfolding. In Midway the observer is also participant, making him a subtle influence in the interactions among executives. Beginning in influence as well as documentation, Scott's role has ended in knowledge and friendship. "Over and over again I found out that there was a good reason for everything that happened," Scott said. "And both Jaffe and his marketing vice president are people I still consider good friends."

Written 17 years ago but still relevant today, Midway symbolizes a special success at the Business School. The victorious components are simple and rare—a willing and able manager, a teacher dedicated to the evolution of his discipline, and a sensitive and thorough casewriter. Simple and rare, the components are also mutually necessary. Midway is Midway because of them.

• • •

Right before my 1st lecture at the HBS I spent most of the night re-reading the case studies and reviewing what I was going to say. I think I slept about 2 hours and was worried that I wouldn't wake up in time.

It was a new and rather daunting experience for me. While I had sat in the amphitheater classroom before, I never was down in front with a couple of hundred students in the Advanced Management course waiting for words of wisdom. Truly a special experience.

Well I knew my subject pretty well and, of course was not reluctant to talk about myself. After all, they had to listen!

It was really exciting for me, and fun. I had a lot to talk about and the opportunity to draw diagrams and graphs on the blackboard. I always started by saying I was sort of like the brother that the hillbilly said was at Harvard. When he was asked how someone from this background could be at Harvard the hillbilly said, "Oh yes he's got two heads and they've got him in a bottle." It was good for a laugh and eased my beginning to talk about the various problems and solutions of a Chief Executive Officer.

Dean Fouraker and Bruce Scott with Natalie and Jeff

Jeff lecturing at the Harvard Business School

Professor Levitt—2nd Row, Right

C. Roland Christensen in Class.
Dedicated to the evolution of his discipline.

Dean Fouraker presents the Award
to Jeff Jaffe. The school showed special
appreciation for a benefactor.

Bruce Scott
Sensitive and
thorough case
writer.

HOW SWEET IT IS

HARVARD UNIVERSITY

GRADUATE SCHOOL OF BUSINESS ADMINISTRATION

GEORGE F. BAKER FOUNDATION

THEODORE LEVITT
Professor of Business Administration

SOLDIERS FIELD
BOSTON, MASSACHUSETTS 02163
(617) 495-6298

May 3, 1976

Mr. Jeff Jaffe
President
Schrafft's Candy Company
Sullivan Square
Boston, Massachusetts 02129

Dear Jeff:

After class last Friday I encountered two groups of PMD students on my way to the office, and in both cases we chatted about what had happened in the class.

The overwhelming messages I got were:

1. Jaffe was a real <u>man</u>—taking all that critical abuse in the class discussion with such ease and aplomb and good cheer when he got a chance to talk.

2. He didn't try to rationalize or apologize or pontificate. He was self-controlled, modest, analytical, and yet cheerful and pleasant.

3. He accepted blame and guilt without apology or excuse. And he didn't try to justify what had been criticized by the class.

4. He was articulate, quick, and pleasant.

I think when the class stood up and applauded at such length at the end, this is what they were saying. And I felt the same way.

Thanks again ever so much.

I'll call in late June or July for a plant tour.

Best wishes,

TL:pm

CHAPTER 24

ACTING CEO

Milford, CT
1977-1980

---

reative Output's output was truly creative. It was started and owned by four Israelis who could never agree on anything. Creative had branches in England, Spain, Israel, and Connecticut in the U.S. Their creative output was prodigious by any standard.

Eliyahu M. Goldratt was the creator of a manufacturing control process which was considered better than the famous Japanese "Just-In-Time" system. (That system, incidentally, was designed by an American automotive engineer who was a consultant to a Japanese company.)

Eli, a brilliant planner of manufacturing processes, was also a charismatic speaker and was sought after by many institutions for his illuminating lectures. However, he was not a good manager, and was difficult to work with.

Business Week magazine in its November 26, 1984 issue wrote "Eli Goldratt is the supremely confident—some would say brash—37-year-old Israeli physicist who invented OPT-Optimized Production Technology." This is a two-part package: a simulated manufacturing program and a set of radical shop-floor management rules which enable companies to increase output while simultaneously lowering its inventory and operating expenses. Companies ranging from Caterpillar Tractor to Bendix and Westinghouse have found that OPT can drastically reduce work-in-progress inventory and increase production. Ironically, some clients say that one of the biggest obstacles Creative Output faces in gaining new disciples is the overly zealous Goldratt himself. Says one colleague "he tends to come in and hit people over the head with a two-by-four." Nonetheless, he even had General Motors as a client.

There was dissention between the owners of Creative Output. Three of the owners actually did not work at the company. But the real problem was that the operation was losing money. To focus on the future, they decided to bring in Barry Wish, an experienced financial planner to advise them. Barry was also a acquirer of corporations in his own right.

Barry brought me in as a Director and due to the dismal management situation, the Directors asked me to take over as Acting President.

This was indeed an industry about which I had no experience. However I was a graduate architectural engineer and always enjoyed a challenge. More important, the directors had confidence in me as a competent manager with a record of successful turnarounds. It was difficult to get Eli to coordinate and work with other members of the staff, but constant pressure improved the situation. Whatever management skills I may have had were tested to the limit at Creative

Output. I commuted to Milford, Connecticut for over a year, and with the cooperation of most of the staff, was able to tone down the management chaos. It was not a lot of fun. In due course, a new president, appropriate to that industry, was elected.

CHAPTER 25

BANKING

Staten Island, N.Y.
1978-1983

S ometimes people tend to forget that Staten Island, that lost and forgotten borough of New York City is actually an island, fairly distant from the other boroughs that comprise New York. It is tethered to the city by the Verrazano Bridge which rivals the Golden Gate Bridge in beauty and grandeur. Touching the south shore of Brooklyn, it is the path for the thousands of pounding feet beginning the annual New York City Marathon.

It is the home of the Community National Bank and Trust Company, a small billion dollar institution held in high regard by the Dutch and Italian residents.

I was elected a director, basically sponsored by Stanley Shaw.

Stan was and still is, an attorney based in nearby Long Island. He is a smart, snappy lawyer who is also a nice guy and runs a prestigious firm with myriad connections to the politics and operations of the area. I am delighted to call him a friend. Although not a banker,

I had a lot of experience from the other side of the table. This enabled me to participate fully in my directorial activities. The work of the bank was typical, old-fashioned personal banking and trust responsibilities.

Unfortunately, the board had to ask the president to resign because of some problems, and it took place immediately. I was asked to become acting president and CEO and took over the reins. The staff was competent and experienced and it was not difficult to maintain operations in a stable and profitable manner.

An interesting activity was a contract with the Triborough Bridge and Tunnel Authority to pick up, count and credit the billion dollars of tolls they collected each year. Have you ever seen a billion dollars—in quarters?

A new president was hired and control of the bank was bought by a wealthy entrepreneur from Thailand. It seems that everyone in Thailand is either starving or is a billionaire.

It so happened that Natalie and I were scheduled to take a trip to the Far East and we were invited to have dinner when we got to Bangkok. Due to a serious glitch in communications, the English-speaking coordinator did not pick us up at the proper time. When he did arrive, we were almost an hour late for the dinner in a special private room of one of the best, swankiest restaurants in Bangkok. We were greeted with hostile stares by the Governor of the Bank of Thailand, the Minister of Defense, several other bankers and their wives, the English speaking Chinese coordinator and his Caucasian girlfriend.

We ate at a large round table—eighteen of us—centered with a huge lazy susan. After formal greetings, platters of seafood and hors d'ouerves were placed on the table and our host proudly announced "Jeff, we have especially brought in some oysters from the unpolluted waters of Phuquet." Well, I hate oysters! In my entire life I have only eaten one. But because of the unwitting insult of our late arrival, I felt that I had to eat some of the oysters from "the unpolluted waters of Phuquet." I managed two and the next morning went to Singapore where I spent the next four days in bed with a 104-degree temperature. Fortunately, Natalie had declined the oysters and we later found that the only other person who became ill was the Caucasian girlfriend.

Banking has such dangerous perils!

CHAPTER 26

TASTY

> **Newark, N.J.**
> **1982**

As far east as one can go and still remain in Newark, lies a small enclave. It is in the shadow of the New Jersey Turnpike and is bordered by four railroad lines roughly forming a square little more than a mile in any direction.

They call it IRONBOUND.

Most of its residents are Portugese, who are handsome, happy, hardworking and devoted to self-governing and self-protection. The nefarious reputation of Newark stops at its borders.

There are three fine restaurants serving gargantuan meals of Spanish/ Portuguese food, washed down by copious quantities of delicious, fruity Sangria wine.

In the middle stands Bernan Foods, producer of 40 varieties of Barney's frozen, kosher hors d'oerves, sold primarily to institutional food wholesalers who then distributed them to restaurants, clubs, and other institutions.

Along with a partner, I bought the business in 1982 and was, as usual, CEO. My family and I moved back to Manhattan.

I didn't much like the hour-long commute through the traffic-laden Lincoln or Holland Tunnels, but it was my nature to be a "hands on" president, especially in a situation like this.

On the very first day, my very first act was to have someone bring me some stuffed derma, a product somewhat like turkey stuffing, which I had always liked, but never had an opportunity to eat. I put it on a plate to begin sampling all of our products over several days. At that point, I swear to you, the world stopped spinning until the permanently assigned rabbi took the forbidden category dish, which I had used, and buried it in the dirt outside. I was learning the business. Actually, the kosher designation had ceased being of paramount importance. The business was profitable even during President Jimmy Carter's 20% interest rate.

Mike Midler, one of the previous owners of Bernan Foods accepted my invitation to remain with the company. He was smart, energetic, very personable and was ideal as Vice President of Sales.

We eventually sold the business at a nice profit.

Bernan Foods

Bernan Foods
Newark, N.J.

CHAPTER 27

PRETTY PERFECT

> **Sailfish Point, FL**
> **February, 1988**

C linging precipitously to the edge, the Hutchinson Islands steadfastly protect the Florida mainland from the relentless pounding, pounding, pounding of the ocean surf. North Hutchinson is about fifty miles long running south from Sebastian to the Fort Pierce inlet.

From there, South Hutchinson continues south for about 30 miles culminating in a 530-acre bulge. The road is a very narrow strip. In some places it is only about 150 yards between the ocean and the inland waterway.

On this bulge, in 1980, the cash cow of Mobil Oil Co. developed a wonderful community. There were one and a half miles of pristine beach, a deep-water marina, tennis courts, a Jack Nicklaus golf course and a beautiful, modern clubhouse practically floating in the ocean. With its own water supply, security force and over 500 residences, it was, indeed, a tiny city. They named it Sailfish Point.

Stuart, its mainland neighbor, claims to be "The Sailfish Capital of the World."

To get to Sailfish Point from the social mecca of Palm Beach, the route goes straight north on truck-crowded Interstate 95 for about 20 miles to Stuart. To get to Sailfish Point you have to travel four miles through the town and finally three miles south over what, if it were Japanese, would be called the Road of 23 Curves. It is probably less than 20 miles as the crow flies, but light years away in style and sophistication. Speaking of crows, Palm Beach is inhabited by lots of crows—old crows who would not deign to go to such a distant outpost as Sailfish Point, fly or drive.

Palm Beach is a beautiful, perfectly manicured, mansion-crowded small town social center of the east coast of Florida. The houses are jealously guarded by a plethora of bougainvillea and hedges. These hedges were something truly special. They were sculpted to magnificent heights, shapes and designs, of which even the most creative hedge could never dream of attaining. A goodly number of the residents are widows. They are rich beyond belief. All of them, either widowed or married, are mostly interested in the next ball or party. There seems to be a different party every night.

Then the old crows turn into elegant peacocks, dripping in diamonds and svelty sheathed in Fiandaca gowns.

The many functions are inevitably organized to make generous donations to worthy charities, but there has always been a slim suspicion that they justify another visit to Alfred and his Fiandaca couture. The main shopping street is the world renowned Worth Avenue. There are those who think that the name should be changed to Net Worth Avenue.

Mobil had a captive Board of Directors, which operated Sailfish until transition took place and the residents took over. The residents elected the Board of Directors and the rule was that the resident who got the most votes became President.

To my great shock I received the most votes and was now President. I was not running for President or any other office. It never crossed my mind. I didn't want to be President, but there was no way that I could reasonably refuse to serve.

I immediately increased the Board to fifteen from seven. More Directors meant more participation and better understanding of the needs and desires of the residents. And better communication.

Surely one of my most significant achievements was the ability to get three top, type A achievers to work with me at Sailfish. Hal Hansen, Jim Spiegel and Sonny Nelson were proven leaders and were instrumental in the results of our work and negotiations with Mobil. They were smart, dedicated and fun, and we made a great team In addition, I was able to get Don McCutcheon, the former head of the Prudential Insurance Co. to serve on my Board. It is not often that a CEO of that stature would be willing to be on a POA Board. He was a great help and was a convincing defense witness for us in the lawsuit that a very small group of six residents brought against us. They seemed to think that my purchase of Parcel M next to the clubhouse for $875,000 was too much, in spite of an appraisal of $1,200,000. It was the only site available for a much needed, and ultimately constructed, expanded pool and beach club restaurant. There were several other minor issues disputing proper governance by the Board and Officers. The verdict by Judge Cynthia Angelos was that every finding was totally in favor of the Board and Officers.

Hal and Jim each became President and Sonny became Secretary. She was the smartest one of all of us.

Allan Golden was always helpful with wise advice and probably devoted more time to various committees than anyone else.

It was a contentious time. Both groups—the residents and Mobil—had many conflicting desires, and the residents were deeply divided amongst themselves. The first year of my presumed two year presidency was devoted to carefully changing the Mobil operations to one wherein the residents needs and wishes were accommodated. Then there were various takeover targets. These included the marina, the real estate office and sales operation, the water and sewer system, parcel M—the large vacant lot next to the clubhouse, beach erosion, pond and lake sanitation, security, roads, and clubhouse maintenance and activities. The golf club was a separate entity.

Negotiating with Mobil was like both parties were sitting on the same side of the table. It was not that they were particularly unfair, but the residents negotiating team I headed had no real leverage.

There were countless meetings over the next two years.

Although I was personally in favor of limited terms of two years for officers, I was strongly requested to serve a third year as President in as much as the negotiations were in mid-course and proceeding satisfactorily.

A critical issue arose when Mobil received an offer to sell the Marina to an outside group. This would have been devastating to the residential integrity of Sailfish Point which was rigidly gate-controlled and monitored.

When Mobil indicated that they were considering that sale, Spiegel and I arranged to get the money and quickly reacted by offering to match the $500,000 proposed price. It was accepted and the Marina became part of the transition package.

The highlight of the transition package was the purchase of the Sailfish Point Real Estate Co.—on an earn-out basis.

I was aware of the numbers of the captive real estate operation, and felt it was very important for the residents to own it.

After lengthy and tedious negotiations, an agreement was reached that Sailfish would take over ownership and operations of the real estate immediately as part of the transition package. Profits of the real estate would be split 50-50 annually between Mobil and Sailfish for the next five years. The net result of this compromise resulted in Mobil receiving $1,000,000 in cash for the sale of the real estate company with Sailfish also obtaining $1,000,000 in cash.

It was interesting that many residents thought that Sailfish actually paid $1,000,000 for the real estate, when the fact was it received $1,000,000 cash to take it over. The money received went immediately into Sailfish coffers and reduced the annual operating costs for the residents.

CHAPTER 28

YOUNG AND PRESIDENT

New York—1951
Russia—1970

When Ray Hickok was 27 years old, his father died. In 1945, this catapulted him into the president's seat of the highly regarded Hickok Company. Many executives in the 40's era would likely be wearing a Hickok belt, pocketing a Hickok wallet or flashing their Hickok cufflinks.

Young and lonely, Ray felt distant from his own company's board of directors. He pondered if he might be able to unite young leaders of his generation into a mutually supportive organization. "Why not bring together presidents who had like problems and like interests," he said. He canvassed the country and found 56 young presidents who were under 40, the nucleus of what would be called the YPO— the Young Presidents Organization.

I heard about YPO in 1951, and became interested in joining what seemed to be an unique group of individuals and possibly a very productive organization. Fortunately, I qualified for membership since we had over $1,000,000* in sales and 100 employees and I was still under 40 years of age. Natalie and I (it was a very spouse-inclusive group) went to our first YPO convention at the famous Frank Lloyd Wright designed Arizona Biltmore in Phoenix. That first meeting began what is now a 60-year association with YPO and CEO, its "graduate" organization. Membership in YPO was terminated at the age of fifty but interest was so high that a new organization, named the Chief Executives Organization was ultimately formed.

I was elected as a director of YPO for two separate three-year terms and served variously as National membership chairman, Policy and Procedure chairman as well as National Treasurer.

Each year there was an annual convention—the YPO University for Presidents—as well as seminars, forums and trips. One of the most noteworthy trips with YPO was a two-week tour of Russia in 1970, my last year in YPO. It was fascinating and replete with various changes in arrangements, delays, and miscommunications. We had our own chartered Aeroflot plane and crew for the 70 YPO'ers. In the air on the way to St. Petersburg we were advised that there were only enough double rooms for only half of the total group. The others would have to occupy separate single rooms. I would always wonder which half were winners. There was an unscheduled and unexplained stop in Baku. In Samarkand we were taken to the airport but not allowed to board the plane. We sat on the tarmac for over two hours in the 100-degree heat sheltered only by the shade offered under the wings of the aircraft.

When in Moscow at the beginning, I requested a tour of a Russian candy factory. A tour guide informed me, with some bravado, that "because Henry Ford didn't allow them to visit his automobile factory, I would not be allowed to see a candy factory in Russia."

---

*$8,245,000 in 2009 dollars—AIER

YPO Banquet, L-R: Sally Hickok, Nat Finkelstein, Jeff Jaffe, Lola Finkelstein, Ray Hickok (founder of YPO), Natalie Jaffe

For reasons which I have never understood, they changed their minds when we got to Kiev. With Len Wolf, a candy distributor and his wife Alice, we were taken on a tour of a candy factory.

Our tour ended in the manager's office where he quickly retrieved a bottle of good brandy from the bottom drawer of his desk. We all had to go through a series of toasts until we practically emptied the bottle. The factory machinery was antiquated and the plant was very labor intensive. The product was not top quality and could never be successfully sold in the United States.

We enjoyed many YPO and CEO universities, forums, and conventions as well as tours in Russia, Germany, and Australia/New Zealand. YPO became a source of many friendships, mutual exchanges of business considerations and participation in meetings, seminars, and conventions, all of which contributed to YPO being the single most outside influence in our lives. At one seminar held at the offices of Johnson and Johnson the pharmaceutical manufacturer, we had an address by General Johnson, the head of the company. After the speech, as was the custom, a number of YPO'ers gathered around the General to ask questions. He answered them very nicely and then commented that his company and YPO companies did not have much in common because of the thousands of employees he had. He then turned to one YPO'er and, in a rather patronizing manner, asked him how many employees he had. It so happened that the person he spoke to was Tom Bata of the Bata Shoe Company. With out batting an eye, Tom responded "30,000 General."

At a CEO nostalgia Seminar in Washington, D.C. John Templeton, the famous financial investor and head of the Templeton Funds explained about the "Laws of Life" contest which he started in his Tennessee hometown county. It consisted of essays written by high school students about what can be the good characteristics of life. Unlike most prizes for students, instead of scholarships, the Laws of Life winners received large cash prizes.

This piqued my interest, and after further conversations with John I decided that it would be good for Martin County where we lived in the winter. We had become casually friendly with John. I recall being at a convention in Berlin, Germany along with John. A few days later we toured the former Nazi government building together. John Templeton was a brilliant man, and beside his fantastic financial success was devoting his life to the encouragement of character, religion, and philanthropy. It was, indeed, a great pleasure to have had the opportunity of some private conversations with him.

The contests were well received in Martin County. Judges included the Mayor of Stuart, Publisher of the Stuart News, Superintendent of the Board of Education, Commissioner of Martin County and myself.

The winners were invited to a non-alcoholic cocktail party but did not know which prize they won until it was announced. The cash prizes were eventually awarded. Each teacher of the winners also received a small cash award.

SPRING
2000

Jeff Jaffe Funds First Martin County *Laws of Life* Essay Contest

At a recent Chief Executives Organization (CEO) meeting in Washington, D.C. Jeff Jaffe heard Sir John Templeton speak about the *Laws of Life* Essay Contest. CEO is a graduate organization of the Young Presidents Organization, an international forum for the exchange of ideas among corporate presidents. At that time Sir John invited all of his friends in CEO to sponsor the contest in their own local community.

Jeff Jaffe

Jeff Jaffe, former CEO of numerous confectionery and food companies, was impressed with the program. After speaking with Sir John, Mr. Jaffe decided to sponsor a *Laws of Life* Essay Contest in Martin County, Florida. His initial contact with the local high schools, the *Stuart News*, the Board of County Commissioners, and the School District was enthusiastically received.

The first Martin County *Laws of Life* Essay Contest took place in January, 2000. More than three hundred essays were submitted from two high schools and three alternative schools, including one boot camp. The awards were presented at a reception in Stuart, Florida on April 10. Thirteen finalists won cash prizes and trophies, and the teacher of each winner also received a cash award. Invited guests included the Superintendent of Schools, the Publisher of the *Stuart News*, County Commissioners, the Mayor of Stuart, and a Martin County Judge.

The cash awards of over $5,000 and all other expenses were entirely funded by Jeff Jaffe. Mr. Jaffe has made an enthusiastic commitment to providing high school students with the opportunity to delineate their values, ideals, and personal goals and share them with other students, parents, teachers, and members of the community.

Editor's note: I was delighted to attend Martin County's very first Laws of Life *Awards Ceremony. I wish you could all have seen the expressions of joy and excitement on the winners' faces as their names and places were announced— what a special evening and what a wonderful tribute to the community of Martin County!*

—*Peggy Veljkovic*

Photo courtesy Deborah Silver/The Stuart News

The top finalists in the Martin County Laws of Life *Essay Contest surround Nicole Kuncl (blue dress, white cardigan) who won First Place ($2,000). They are, clockwise from top left: Kristy Reid, who won Honorable Mention ($100); Nicole Larese, who won Honorable Mention ($100); Daniel Felter, who won Honorable Mention ($100); Caroline Neary, who won Honorable Mention ($100), Alfred Miller III, who won Third Place ($500); Shannon Matheny, who won Honorable Mention ($100); Stephanie Schect, who won Fourth Place ($300); Leighan Howard, who won Second Place ($1,000) and Jose Farinos, who won Honorable Mention ($100).*

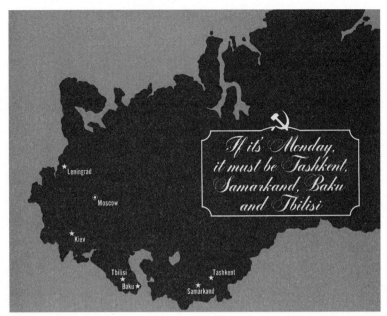

If it's Monday,
it must be Tashkent,
Samarkand, Baku
and Tbilisi

YPO in the USSR 1970

EDITOR'S NOTE: This report was written by, and primarily for, the participants in the 1970 YPO Soviet Union Seminar. Editing a document written by perhaps sixty people poses many unique problems. Not the least is to give proper credit to each reporter. When there was no duplicate coverage, the author's name is so indicated. In the majority of cases, however, the articles represent a compilation of the work of two or more persons, hence all of the names are listed together. (This significantly increases the already high risk of bodily injury to the editor.) Inconsistencies of tense and person have not been eliminated where necessary to make a point, and every effort has been made to retain the flavor of each individual style. Inasmuch as this trip means many different things to many different travellers, brevity in this report is not a criteria. Cost is!

Read this journal with the understanding that it is not intended to be a best seller, but to simply record our travels and impressions. Editing it has enabled me to relive many happy experiences. You will too, as you read the words of your "fellow travellers".

Russian candy factory—Kiev—Jeff behind Alice Wolf, Russian
plant manager, Len Wolf behind Natalie

CHAPTER 29

PRODUCING CHOCOLATE

Philadelphia, PA
1969

A man named Blumenthal started making chocolate in the United States in 1911. That was four generations ago. His two sons took over from him and were followed by their four sons. There were brothers Bud and Joe and their cousins, brothers Jack and Sam, who ran the business from the 1940's on. At least one son joined them in the business making the fourth generation.

The cousins didn't seem to like each other very much and operated on a "mind your own business—I'll mind mine." Bud, the president, would spend his mornings cutting cocoa beans and was responsible for the vitally important purchasing of cocoa beans. This was the critical job, because without the proper cocoa beans, good chocolate would not be available. Joe and Sam handled the sales and marketing of their product. At the same time, Jack was responsible for the manufacturing. No one was really the boss and all decisions were ruled by negotiation, where departmental self-interest prevailed.

It was a rather difficult management process, but it worked, most of the time.

Although started as a producers of industrial chocolate (selling chocolate to the actual producers of candy) they managed to slip into the consumer candy business as well. Blumenthal was the company that shipped the alleged salmonella to Chunky.

It was a reasonable profitable operation, but wasn't going anywhere. I was primarily interested in their consumer products like Goobers, Raisinets, Sno-Caps, and several others. There was significant synergism available and that favorably impacted the bottom line. However the Blumenthal company had the capability to manufacture the chocolate we used even when it was growing substantially. I was aware of the unique place Blumenthal had in the confectionery trade, producing chocolate for other manufacturers while selling a consumer product as well. This unusual operation rounded out a very positive vertical manufacturing base.

As part of Ward Foods, we had no trouble raising the cash for the purchase. I became CEO of Blumenthal and during the first year spent two days each week in Philadelphia. Virtually all the personnel were retained in place and were cooperative.

The Robert A. Johnston Co., located in Milwaukee manufactured chocolate, and cookies and cakes. The product line fit in well with the Ward Candy and Chocolate group. I took over as CEO in 1969, spent two days a week there for five months, and merged it into the Group without difficulty. The Johnston plant was old but efficient. There were 350 employees and they added a welcome vertical dimension to our manufacturing by producing chocolate from cocoa beans. Tucked away in a small room on the fifth floor, four little old ladies were employed in unhurriedly making Graham Cracker Pie Crusts which was soon sold at a fine profit.

Simple Simon Frozen Pies in Los Angeles was acquired in 1967, Superior Potato Chips in Detroit in 1970 and Quinlan Pretzel Company, Reading PA in 1971.

CHAPTER 30

PROBABLY A MISTAKE

> **Biltmore Hotel, NYC**
> **1964**

I was the recipient of two industry awards. They were the AMCC—Association of Manufacturers of Candy and Chocolate and the Kettle Award from Candy Industry.

The AMCC held a testimonial dinner at the Biltmore Hotel in March 1964 attended by over 400 manufacturers, suppliers, associates and media. The award was presented by U.S. Congressman Herbert Tenzer.

My speech centered on a unique—for 1964—concern. Here are some excerpts:

"We live in a world that soon may not have a candy industry. What will cause a billion-dollar industry to disappear? Figures show that fewer and fewer companies are doing more and more of the business. Enterprises that were once independent—small, medium and large—have become divisions of giant corporations where candy is a side interest. Of course, I am not even against mergers and acquisitions, as some of you may have suspected all along. But if the trend continues there will no longer be room in our industry for the innovative entrepreneurs like Milton Hershey, Frank Mars, Frank Brach, Otto Schnering, George Williamson and others.

"The same thing is happening elsewhere. In automobiles, beer, bakeries, grocery stores and oil, we hear the same story." We seem to be racing to the ultimate development of one Super National Food Manufacturing Company which will sell all of its output to the Super National Supermarket Company, all of which will be controlled in Washington by the Super National Bureaucrat. We may find that we have lost Free Enterprise and backed our way into a socialist or corporate state!"

"I was a shirt-sleeved plower of fields. I sowed details and harvested decisions. I was a businessman and that meant I had to create jobs and make profits. To do that I had to have a climate of competition and free enterprise, something we should never forget."

The Kettle Award
Reprinted from Candy Industry Magazine
July 1971

Kettle winner is active, committed candy leader

Jeff Jaffe, the 1971 Candy Man of the Year and the 26th Kettle Award winner, is a versatile businessman and humanitarian who is deeply involved in candy industry activities and community affairs.

Recently named to the board of directors of Ward Foods, Mr. Jaffe is the president of Ward's Chocolate, Candy and Biscuit Group which he was instrumental in organizing. The group consists of the Chunky, Schutter and Blumenthal operations, Williamson Candy Co. (a new acquisition), and the Robert A. Johnson Co. and Farm Crest Cookies subsidiaries (formerly part of Ward's Snack Division).

Among Mr. Jaffe's major responsibilities is coordinating the operations of seven plants across the country and overseeing the activities of a number of sales groups.

Of major importance in the coming months will be an internal growth program with emphasis on developing better productivity and marketing techniques, Mr. Jaffe told CSI recently.

"We will be looking into methods for increasing our distribution system so that we can put our products into more outlets," he noted.

Mr. Jaffe is well qualified to handle his present responsibilities having had experience in production and plant improvement,

sales and marketing, financial techniques and product quality advancement prior to coming to Ward. He has been in the candy industry for over 20 years, serving as advertising manager, Sweets Co. of America, president and chairman of the board of The Chunky Corp. and the Schutter Candy Co. He became president of Ward Candy Co. in 1969.

In addition to applying his sales and marketing expertise to his own company's operations, Mr. Jaffe has been active in the affairs of the Association of Manufacturers of Confectionery and Chocolate. He has served as a director for many years and was president of the group from 1959 to 1961. He is also active in the Candy Executives Club, and served as a director of the group from 1956 to 1959.

Mr. Jaffe has always been interested in candy industry / government relationships and has worked with the Federal government to set up a salmonella prevention code.

In addition to participating in industry activities, Mr. Jaffe has been involved in community affairs. He is past treasurer and a longtime national director of the Young Presidents Organization. His interest in education has brought him to Harvard's Graduate School of Business Administration where he has been a guest lecturer for the past seven years.

Jeff Jaffe

He participates in local government activities in Hewlett Bay Park, N. Y., where he resides with his wife Natalie and two daughters. He has been treasurer of the Village of Hewlett Bay Park, a member of the United Fund Community Chest, and chairman of the building campaign for Temple Sinai.

Tall, lean, charming, with a quick friendly smile, Mr. Jaffe seems constantly in motion be he making company decisions, visiting foreign countries to explore their candy plants or meet community leaders, or participating in his own community's activities.

His endless efforts on behalf of his industry and community and his warm relationships with his employees and friends are once again being publicly recognized as Jeff. Jaffe is named 1971 Candy Man of the Year.

AMCC Testimonial Dinner for Jaffe—1964

Natalie, Holly, Bonnie and Jeff at AMCC Dinner—1964

COMBINATION clock-barometer is presented to Jeff Jaffe (l.) at recent AMCC testimonial by Leonard Wurzel. (See page 36.)

Jaffe: mergers may kill candy industry

The current merger trend may result in disappearance of the candy industry as it is known today, warned Jeff Jaffe, president of The Chunky Corp., Brooklyn, N.Y. at a testimonial dinner in his honor in New York. (See page 36 for his talk.)

The testimonial sponsored by the Association of Manufacturers of Confectionery and Chocolate, was attended last month by some 400 industry members.

Leonard Wurzel, AMCC president, introduced a previous recipient of the honor, Congressman Herbert Tenzer, who spoke about Mr. Jaffe's many accomplishments.

Mr. Jaffe is the youngest executive ever to be honored by the organization

CANDY INDUSTRY and CONFECTIONERS JOURNAL

April 7, 1964

CHAPTER 31

REFLECTIONS

1950-2010

I'm not really one to look back a lot, but as George Santayana said, "He who cannot remember history is condemned to repeat it."

It is an opportunity to learn, review and proceed forward a little wiser.

My business career was varied, fun, and especially interesting. Unintentionally it included a number of "turnarounds." Turnarounds are often hazardous and dangerous. Turning an unprofitable company into a money-making enterprise depended on the ability of the "turnarounder"—that unique entrepreneurial character who must spend his time round the clock fixing the acquired company. Timing, luck and determination are important. But it will all fail without the entrepreneur offering the critical, intelligent solution.

Thanks to my forefathers I grew up in America, that is, the United States of America. It offered me the opportunity to have a full education, freedom of choice, opportunity and encouragement in a wide open, expansive country where the potholes were surmountable and the hills fairly shallow.

As in each civilization, society has risks in its inexorable continuum of hard work, dedication, constructive philosophy, legal observance as it then existed, frugality and good will.

I was able to observe, learn and achieve at whatever rate my determination and desire was willing to exert. I was very fortunate to have the strength, wisdom, and the good fortune of help from the right people at the right time.

I was very happy to be one tiny shred of proof of Newton's first law: "A body in motion tends to stay in motion." This applies to people as well as inaminate objects, and my activities have kept me in constant motion. I love it!

All of this can be called trite or banal—something worn out by constant use, or no longer having its original freshness and impressive force. But that very implication clearly guarantees and emphasises the truth and reality it espouses.

Everyone has problems. Every situation is imperfect. Mine happened to be very notable. They were actually setbacks. But every adversity I faced was ultimately overcome. More important, it always seemed to lead to further accompishments.

There is not much I would want to have had differently. Losing a small fortune wasn't very palatable, but I made it back and more in the following years.

It resulted in broadening my activities, my experience, and my direction. Don't misunderstand me. I didn't want it, I didn't like it but I had to face up to it. I said at the time, "How many times do I have to do it?" And the answer, clearly, was, "As many times as necessary!" I achieved a lot of growth.

Again, "If it doesn't kill you, it makes you stronger."

REFLECTIONS

Between golf and business, I spent a lot of time away from home, which, of course, meant less time with my family. I'm not sure what the proper balance should have been between family time and time for the business of providing the necessities of life and nurturing of family, as well as time for my own personal, and very necessary, achievement of career activities.

I am very fortunate indeed to reach my 90th birthday and our 65th Wedding Anniversary, of which I keep telling Natalie is still a trial marriage. A combination of good genes, moderation and luck.

Am I satisfied? Well, almost. I'm happy with what I have accomplished, but there could have been more. Yes, there always can be more.

APPENDIX

TELL IT LIKE IT IS

By DUNAGIN

'Everything was recalled by the Food and Drug Administration.'

JEFF JAFFE
BUSINESS PROFILE
1945-1990

Food Broker—Retail Missionary Salesman

Loft Candy Co.— Candymaker helper
                  Retail stores product supply manager
Tootsie Rolls— Advertising Department
                  Advertising Manager

Chairman, President and principal stockholder
    The Chunky Corporation—from 1950
    Schutter Candy Co.—from 1958
    Klotz Confection Co.—from 1960

President and CEO, Ward Candy Co.
    This company was formed by the acquisition of the Chunky
    Corp. and Schutter Candy Co. by Ward Foods.

President and CEO, Ward Foods Candy, Chocolate & Biscuit Group
    Acquired and merged four candy and chocolate companies, and
    one cookie company, and became the major profit center of
    Ward Foods.

Chairman and CEO, Ward Foods Branded Foods Group
    Group composed of:
        The Chunky Corp   Schutter Candy Co.
        Blumenthal Chocolate Co.   Johnston Frozen Pie Co.
        Robert A. Johnston Co.   Superior Potato Chip Co.
        Quinlan Pretzel Co.   Williamson Candy Co.

President and COO, Ward Foods, Inc.
> Manufacturing and operations in food and food related products. The range included bread, rolls, cake, confectionery and chocolate, meat processing, dairy products, potato chips, pretzels, seafood, and food machinery.

President and CEO, The Schrafft Candy Co
> Vice President, Consumer Products Group, Gulf & Western Industries
>> Manufacturer of complete line of confectionery products utilizing 1,000,000 square feet of factory space in Boston, MA and Reading, PA

Director, Creative Output, Inc.
Acting President
> Designer and supplier of computer related manufacturing control systems to large manufacturers such as General Motors

President and CEO, Bernan Foods
> Manufacturer of frozen hors d'oeuvres

Director, Community National Bank Staten Island
Acting President

Director, The Oxford Energy Co.
> Builder and operator of electric power plants using tires and rice hulls as fuel source

Director, Lyntex Corporation

JEFF JAFFE
OTHER ACTIVITIES

Assoc. of Manufacturers of
Confectionery & Chocolate

Director
President—1959-1961

Candy Executives Club, NY

Director—1956-1959

National Confectioners Assoc.

National Committee—1964

Federation of Jewish Philanthropies

Received Candy Division Service
Award—1962

Young Presidents' Organization

Board of Directors—1956-1959 and
1962-1965
National Treasurer—1963

Harvard University
Graduate School of Business

Guest Lecturer—1963-1979
Special Recognition Award

Woodmere Academy, NY

Trustee—1959-1968

Village of Hewlett Bay Park, NY

Treasurer—1969-1972

Temple Sinai, Woodmere, NY

Chairman—Building Campaign
providing a new Temple

United Fund Community Chest

Co-Chairman Hewlett, L.I.

U.S. Defense Orientation Conference Association	Director
Mayor Robert Wagner's Committee to Combat Juvenile Delinquency, NY	Co-Chairman—1959-1961
Joint Defense Appeal	Chairman Confectionery Division— 1959-1961
Jr. Achievement, NYC	Board of Directors—1958-1961
Kettle Award, Candy Industry	Man of the Year—1971
Sailfish Point Community— Stuart, FL	Director—1990-1997 President—1995-1997 Chairman—1998

On The Rise

Felix A. Juda Photo

NO PLACE TO GO BUT UP. With the razing of its first home on Washington Ave., Lawrence, Temple Sinai builds for the future on the original site. Participating in the goundbreaking cere- monies are building fund chairman Jeff Jaffe of Hewlett Bay Park, wielding the shovel and (from left) Harold Bobroff of Woodmere, Robert Mandel of Cedarhurst, William Immershein of North Woodmere, Stanley Rich of Hewlett, Herbert Gold of Hewlett Harbor and Arthur Silver of Bayside, architect of the new temple building which is scheduled for completion in the spring of 1970.

Mayor Robert Wagner, N.Y.C. City Hall steps—1958

American Institute for Economic Research, a nonprofit, scientific and charitable organization. Great Barrington, Massachusetts 01230

Economic Bulletin, January 2010

Purchasing Power Conversion Factors

	To Convert:			To Convert:			To Convert:	
Year	Past Dollars to 2009 Dollars Use Multiplier A	2009 Dollars to Past Dollars Use Multiplier B	Year	Past Dollars to 2009 Dollars Use Multiplier A	2009 Dollars to Past Dollars Use Multiplier B	Year	Past Dollars to 2009 Dollars Use Multiplier A	2009 Dollars to Past Dollars Use Multiplier B
1920	10.7204	0.0933	1950	8.8966	0.1124	1980	2.6020	0.3843
1921	11.9781	0.0835	1951	8.2465	0.1213	1981	2.3587	0.4240
1922	12.7624	0.0784	1952	8.0909	0.1236	1982	2.2219	0.4501
1923	12.5385	0.0798	1953	8.0303	0.1245	1983	2.1527	0.4645
1924	12.5385	0.0798	1954	7.9706	0.1255	1984	2.0636	0.4846
1925	12.2519	0.0816	1955	8.0003	0.1250	1985	1.9926	0.5018
1926	12.1135	0.0826	1956	7.8827	0.1269	1986	1.9563	0.5112
1927	12.3223	0.0812	1957	7.6302	0.1311	1987	1.8874	0.5298
1928	12.5385	0.0798	1958	7.4190	0.1348	1988	1.8124	0.5518
1929	12.5385	0.0798	1959	7.3680	0.1357	1989	1.7291	0.5783
1930	12.8388	0.0779	1960	7.2435	0.1381	1990	1.6405	0.6096
1931	14.1058	0.0709	1961	7.1709	0.1395	1991	1.5742	0.6352
1932	15.6503	0.0639	1962	7.0996	0.1409	1992	1.5282	0.6544
1933	16.4930	0.0606	1963	7.0068	0.1427	1993	1.4838	0.6739
1934	16.0006	0.0625	1964	6.9164	0.1446	1994	1.4468	0.6912
1935	15.6503	0.0639	1965	6.8066	0.1469	1995	1.4069	0.7108
1936	15.4251	0.0648	1966	6.6176	0.1511	1996	1.3665	0.7318
1937	14.8895	0.0672	1967	6.4194	0.1558	1997	1.3359	0.7486
1938	15.2063	0.0658	1968	6.1612	0.1623	1998	1.3154	0.7602
1939	15.4251	0.0648	1969	5.8422	0.1712	1999	1.2870	0.7770
1940	15.3149	0.0653	1970	5.5260	0.1810	2000	1.2451	0.8031
1941	14.5856	0.0686	1971	5.2940	0.1889	2001	1.2107	0.8260
1942	13.1539	0.0760	1972	5.1294	0.1950	2002	1.1918	0.8391
1943	12.3936	0.0807	1973	4.8290	0.2071	2003	1.1653	0.8582
1944	12.1823	0.0821	1974	4.3491	0.2299	2004	1.1350	0.8810
1945	11.9116	0.0840	1975	3.9853	0.2509	2005	1.0978	0.9109
1946	10.9953	0.0909	1976	3.7682	0.2654	2006	1.0635	0.9403
1947	9.6147	0.1040	1977	3.5381	0.2826	2007	1.0341	0.9670
1948	8.8966	0.1124	1978	3.2885	0.3041	2008	0.9958	1.0042
1949	9.0088	0.1110	1979	2.9533	0.3386	2009	1.0000	1.0000

How to Convert Past and Present Values

The table above provides a simple way to convert values from the past into their equivalent value today (or vice versa). To convert a value from a particular year to its 2009 equivalent, simply multiply the original price by the conversion factor Multiplier A shown in the table for the appropriate year.

For instance, say you want to know if the value of your house has

the original price of the house by the Multiplier A factor shown for the year you purchased it.

Example: A house was purchased in 1965 for $25,000. Adjusting for price inflation, this price in terms of 2009 dollars is $25,000 x 6.8066 = $170,165. This is approximately how much the house would have to sell for today just to keep up with price inflation.

dollars, simply multiply today's dollar amount by the conversion factor Multiplier B shown in the table for the appropriate year.

Example: If the price of a movie ticket is about $7 today, what was the constant-dollar equivalent in, say, 1974? Today's $7 purchase price in terms of 1974 dollars is $7 x 0.2299 = $1.61.

HOW SWEET IT IS

Department of Commerce

This Is To Certify: *That* **Irwin Hugh Jaffe**

has satisfactorily completed the following controlled courses of instruction for

Private Pilot

GROUND COURSE
(Minimum—72 hours)

| History | Parachutes | Civil air regulations | Theory of flight | Instrument |
| Meteorology | Aircraft | Practical air navigation | Engines | Radio |

FLIGHT COURSE
(Minimum—17 hours dual, 18 hours solo)

Taxiing	Take-offs	Forced landings	Steep power turns	Power landings
Air work	Landings	Precision landings	Slips—forward, side	Dragging areas
Stalls	Spins	Figure eights	Power approaches	Cross country

and is accorded all the rights and privileges of that grade as evidenced by Certificate of Competency No. 22973-40

Issued this ___30th___ *day of* September ___, 1940

Approved:

Assistant Secretary of Commerce. GPO 16—18848

(GROUND SCHOOL)

(FLIGHT SCHOOL)

CANDY HALL OF FAME INDUCTEES FOR 1977

MANUFACTURER:

JEFF JAFFEE

Jeff Jaffe, President of The Schrafft Candy Company is a distinguished member of the confectionery industry and has been one of its leaders for more than a quarter of a century.

Starting with the creation of Chunky, and the legendary growth of that brand and Company, he then further polished the luster of his career by becoming the architect of Ward Candy's explosive growth and acquisition program.

His accomplishments in making Ward Candy one of the most profitable and fastest growing candy companies in America led to Jeff Jaffe's election, by the Board of Ward Foods, to the presidency of the $400-million parent company.

In 1974, Jaffe took on another exciting challenge – that of rescuing one of America's, and the confectionery industry's, most venerable companies: The Schrafft Candy Company. In less than three years, he has succeeded in nearly doubling the size of Schrafft, and re-establishing it as one of the leaders of the candy industry.

Schrafft's current renaissance is the most eloquent tribute to this leader and statesman of the industry.

Jaffee has been significantly honored by his industry, as well as outside of it. Among many plaudits accorded to him over the years, most recently he was honored by Harvard University in a manner unprecedented even for Harvard. The University singled out his efforts in the field of case development as unique, and greater than any made by anyone in Harvard's long and distinguised history of use and development of the case study method.

With his election to the Hall of Fame, Jeff Jaffe is now the recipient of the industry's three most coveted awards: The Kettle, The AMCC Executive of the Year, and NCSA's Hall of Fame.

National Confectionary Salesmen's Association

1977

Candy Hall of Fame Convention

Flying a jet trainer with Air Force instructor—NORAD 1963

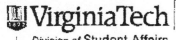

Office of the Commandant
143 Brodie Hall (0213)
Blacksburg, Virginia 24061
540/231-6413 Fax: 540/231-3443
E-mail: vtcorps@vt.edu
www.vtcc.vt.edu

February 28, 2011

MEMORANDUM

TO: Mr. Jeff Jaffe

FROM: Major General Jerrold P. Allen

SUBJECT: Jaffe Eager Squad Awards

Thank you Jeff for initiating and generously supporting the Jaffe Eager Squad Awards. You have significantly enhanced the success of the annual Corps of Cadets drill competition.

The Jaffe Eager Squad trophy, permanent wall plaque, and cash awards have motivated cadets to work hard while training for the competition. You have helped to lead the Corps to much higher standards of professionalism.

Your wonderful support of the Corps and our outstanding cadets epitomizes the motto of Virginia Tech: Ut Prosim, "that I may serve." I am grateful for your leadership and your gifts. You have strengthened and perpetuated a most important Corps of Cadets tradition.

Thank you!

Invent the Future